BUILDING GOOD SOCIAL RELATIONSHIPS

HOW TO CULTIVATE RELATIONSHIPS THAT MATTER FOR PERSONAL GROWTH

FUNCTIONAL HEALTH SERIES

SAM FURY

Copyright SF Nonfiction Books © 2024

www.SFNonfictionBooks.com

All Rights Reserved
No part of this document may be reproduced without written consent from the author.

WARNINGS AND DISCLAIMERS

The information in this publication is made public for reference only.

Neither the author, publisher, nor anyone else involved in the production of this publication is responsible for how the reader uses the information or the result of his/her actions.

CONTENTS

Introduction   vii

Understanding Social Relationships	1
The Foundations of Social Relationships	20
Developing Meaningful Connections	47
The Digital Dimension	72
Navigating Challenges in Relationships	85
Cultivating Professional Relationships	105
Special Relationships and Situations	118
Conclusion	142
Author Recommendations	149
About Sam Fury	151
References	153

THANKS FOR YOUR PURCHASE

Get Your Next SF Nonfiction Book FREE!

Claim the book of your choice at:

https://www.SFNonfictionBooks.com/Free-Book

You will also be among the first to know of all the latest releases, discount offers, bonus content, and more.

Go to:

https://www.SFNonfictionBooks.com/Free-Book

Thanks again for your support.

INTRODUCTION

I define energy as the connection that exists between people when they feel seen, heard, and valued; when they can give and receive without judgement; and when they derive sustenance and strength from the relationship. –Brené Brown

When you think of your social relationships, what comes to mind? Do you feel seen, valued, or heard in your social relationships? Have you taken the time to consider whether or not your social relationships are healthy?

In the last 30 years, the construct surrounding building social relationships has changed, with many of us turning to social media to keep in contact with or build our social relationships. Although technology has many benefits, it also has a few downsides, many of which are centered around our ability to build and maintain strong and healthy relationships. In fact, you can find yourself facing issues such as reduced face-to-face interactions or becoming way too comfortable with online interactions, reducing your capability to create or maintain conversation. With this comes major issues like an inability to be present due to being constantly distracted or aloof. Basically, many of us are facing issues with isolation because of our dependence on technology and because we're all constantly in our own worlds.

Outside of these issues, many of us tend to find ourselves in spaces that make it difficult for us to create actual bonds because of past trauma, which can show up as communication or trust issues. We can also find ourselves battling a balance between our work and our personal lives; whatever the issue is, the common denominator is that building social relationships is hard. In fact, many of us are looking for ways to improve our social relationships. This is because many of us have an innate longing for connection as human beings, which translates to building relationships with others.

When we have social relationships, we also have a sense of belonging, emotional support, improved esteem, improved physical and mental health, and more. A beautiful way to illustrate this is through a quote by Sophie Strand that reads, "Everything is connected to something. But not everything is connected to everything. The differences are vital" (para. 5).

Our social connections can offer us the chance to belong, to be esteemed, and to be part of society. It's all linked to a system that allows us to thrive, meaning that we cannot exist in isolation. By building the fundamentals, we're able to make our lives as fulfilling as we need them to be.

By reading this book and grasping the fundamentals of how to build your social relationships, you afford yourself the luxury of connections that are ultimately and strongly connected to your ability to thrive. In this book, I take a deeper look into the foundations of social relationships, developing meaningful connections, how technology has affected our ability to connect, and more. Come with me as I take us on a deeper journey toward understanding social relationships so that we're able to develop healthy and strong connections, which can have a profound effect on how we live, think, and process our current experiences.

UNDERSTANDING SOCIAL RELATIONSHIPS

Man is by nature a social animal, an individual who is unsocial naturally and not accidentally is either beneath our notice or more than human. Society is something that precedes the individual. –Aristotle

What comes to mind when you think of a thriving and healthy society? Does your mind linger on technology, food, water, or any other basic human need? In each of those mental pictures, what do you find as a common denominator? Are you focused on the need for survival or the human beings who have interacted to create a healthy and thriving society?

When we think of society, we're usually thinking of relationships. Our entire society is built on relationships, whether personal or professional. In fact, we rarely live a life of happiness without human interaction because we're built to socialize.

Isolation has been used as a means of torture because of how it usually results in physical and psychological deterioration and, in some cases, death. Over time, scientists became interested in the effect that social interaction has on people and within communities, businesses, and other spaces where humans have to interact. Their findings suggested and concluded that socialization plays a vital part in our well-being as human beings. The same findings also showed that people who were more socially intertwined were far happier, healthier, and lived longer than those who mostly lived in isolation.

Having social relationships can help improve mental health, lower the risk of things such as anxiety and depression, increase your self-esteem, strengthen your immune system, and more. The amazing thing about healthy social relationships is that they afford us the opportunity to pour into others, meaning that everyone benefits from the connection.

When we don't have healthy social relationships, it can lead to social isolation. Social isolation can be defined as a lack of social engagement or a lack of regular contact with others. Social isolation can lead to things such as increased blood pressure, disrupted sleeping patterns, and an increase in stress levels.

Social isolation is particularly prevalent among the elderly due to their mobility issues. Having issues with mobility can make doing simple things, such as going out to see others, exceedingly difficult. Other underlying issues, such as eye problems, a decrease in overall health, and more, can also play a major role in the ability of the elderly to see others. On the other hand, those who have healthy social relationships have a better quality of life, lower the risk of things such as dementia and mental decline, need less assistance, and can feel satisfied with their overall lives.

The younger generation is also at risk of feeling the repercussions of social isolation on their physical well-being. They are at risk of obesity, inflammation, and higher blood pressure. These can lead to other health complications such as stroke, cancer, heart disease, and more.

When dealing with social isolation, you'll want to understand the difference between loneliness and solitude. Loneliness can be attributed to a lack of social contacts or the inability to engage with others to the degree that allows for healthy social relationships. Solitude is when we are happy and content with our own company. This means that although we can be in contact with others, we're able to sit with ourselves and not feel lonely.

So, what are social relationships, and what is their role in society and within our own lives? What are the different types of relationships, and how do they affect us holistically?

Social Relationships Defined

To define social relationships, we first need to define social relations. Social relations can be defined as engagement or contact, whether voluntary or involuntary, between two or more individuals. Social relationships, on the other hand, are a lot more complex as they deal with already existing or recurring interactions between people. Such relationships can be fostered in families, work spaces, or with neighbors and coworkers; either way, the connection or engagement is happening continuously. When looked at loosely, we can say that social relationships are more voluntary and frequent because we allow those people into our personal spaces.

Different Types of Social Relationships

When dealing with social relationships, you'll need to understand that there are different types of social relationships that all play different roles in our lives and society as a whole. In this section, we take a deeper look into the different types of social relationships.

Before we take a dive into the different types of social relationships, we need to understand how what we're exposed to can have an influence on our social relationships. Below, we briefly explore how what we're exposed to influences our social relationships:

- Family members play a major role in our ability to socialize. This is because family is usually our first point of contact and social interaction. How they teach us to socialize is one of the tools we use to build social relationships.
- Schools are a place where the foundation of socializing is laid. In this environment, we deal with various personalities and learn to form bonds with others. This is also an environment where we solidify our knowledge of authority and consequences outside of our homes.
- The older we become, the more we become focused on building relationships among our peers. When we're teenagers, we transition from relying on our parents to starting the process of finding our feet within society. At this time, we also gain an understanding of the different genders and the roles each gender is meant to play.
- After gaining our independence as teenagers, we also tend to find ourselves in part-time work spaces where we learn to socialize with our colleagues for the first time. From this

point on, we gain a certain understanding or idea of what we're meant to do in the workplace and the different ways we're meant to interact with those we work with.
- Technology and the media as a whole have contributed significantly to our ability to socialize with others. This is because mass media influences how we view the world through the information available to us at the time. Technology, on the other hand, aids the media in spreading messages to the public.
- One of the many things that contributes to our ability to socialize is our religion. This is because each religion or belief system has rules and regulations that each person should be abiding by. These ideologies lay the foundation for our train of thought and what we view as right and wrong. Culture can also play a major role in our ability to create bonds with others.

Now that we understand how our environment plays a role in our ability to create bonds, we need to look into the different types of social relationships and their roles.

Friendships

Friendships can be described as a relationship of mutual connection and affection between individuals. Some may refer to this type of relationship as a platonic relationship that can happen between males and females or within the same gender. The role of this type of relationship is to offer support, mutual connection, companionship, shared experience, emotional connection, and more.

Friendships offer us a safe space to turn to when seeking healthy relationships with others. Through these relationships, we are able to have people who will support us through tough and vulnerable stages of life. The point of these is to offer emotional, mental, and spiritual support, especially when we are in friendship circles that share similar interests and sentiments. Keep in mind that friendships can evolve into romantic relationships.

Romantic Relationships

The term relationship leads us down the path of thinking of romantic relationships when, in truth, relationships have a broad spectrum of other relationships. Romantic relationships can be defined as an interpersonal relationship that often involves emotional or physical closeness between the individuals in the relationship. The characteristics of this type of relationship include things such as physical attraction, commitment, shared values, affection, and more. When we're in romantic relationships, we usually experience things such as intimacy, emotional growth, partnership, love, and more.

When we're in a romantic relationship, we want to fulfill our need for intimacy, social connection, and more. Like all connections, romantic relationships are meant to be nurtured, because what we don't nurture or care for dies. Romantic relationships tend to follow the same process of development and deterioration as other relationships.

Family Relationships

For many of us, the first relationship we're exposed to is usually a family bond or relationship. This relationship will usually set the tone for other relationships and our ability to function within them. Ideally, family relationships are meant to offer us love, support, and care to foster an environment that allows us to maintain familial bonds. We can recognize this type of relationship through blood ties, shared history, obligations, and emotional connections.

Professional Relationships

Professional relationships are usually fostered in professional spaces, such as at a workplace or within a professional online space. The main goal of professional relationships is to collaborate, achieve career goals and objectives, network, and advance in the professional space you acquire. Within this relationship, we can find things such as professionalism, mutual respect, good communication, and shared professional goals.

Acquaintanceship

These are particularly common, especially when we continuously run in the same circles with certain individuals. An acquaintance is someone that we may know by sight or association with other individuals whom we may know; however, we do not know this person on an intimate level.

With an acquaintance, we are not emotionally invested and may share similar interests or connections. We can also find ourselves having casual or limited interactions based on where we may be at the time. The main role of such an interaction could be networking, socializing, or simply exchanging certain information. Whatever the interaction, we aren't as emotionally invested as we would be if we were with our friends.

Many people tend to confuse acquaintances with friendships; however, when we look at the objectives of the relationships, we can see that they are completely different.

Mentorship

To understand the role of a mentorship relationship, we first need to understand what a mentor is and what role they play in our lives. A mentor can be defined as an individual who offers advice, guidance, and help to those who are less experienced in a particular field. A mentor will often offer their skills, expertise, knowledge, and resources to help those that they are in a mentorship relationship with.

Mentorship relationships are meant to provide guidance, help with knowledge sharing, and skills sharing while also assisting the mentee to develop their skills. The mentor is also responsible for helping the mentee in a personal and professional capacity.

The characteristics of such a relationship include advice, feedback, learning, development, and the sharing of expertise.

Neighborly Relationship

This type of relationship is built during our time living in a certain area. Those who live around us or are in close proximity to our homes are known as neighbors. Some may confuse this type of relationship with an acquaintance; however, the goals and characteristics of this relationship are different.

Neighborly relationships are usually centered around neighborly assistance, support, safety, and belonging within that community. The characteristics of that relationship may include things such as digital communication, mutual respect, boundaries, and other things that involve community engagement.

Online Relationships

In today's day and age, online relationships are becoming far more common. An online relationship is when two individuals meet and communicate through digital platforms such as social media or other online platforms. These online relationships can either be romantic or simply revolve around creating and maintaining a friendship.

The main purpose of an online relationship is to create a social connection, exchange information, offer emotional support, or simply create a virtual space that allows for virtual companionship. Either way, the relationship is maintained and created through digital means.

Teacher-Student Relationship

The teacher-student relationship is one of the most common relationships, considering that many of us have been in situations where we needed a teacher. The main goal of this relationship is to impart knowledge, and although this may seem similar to a mentor relationship, the objective of this relationship is different.

A teacher-student relationship is characterized by the teacher offering instruction and guidance on material that the learner is meant to grasp. They will then evaluate how well the learner knows the material and grade them according to what they know. The learner, on the other hand, is meant to seek knowledge and improvement from the teacher while asking questions about what they don't know or understand.

The main goal of this relationship is for the teacher to provide the knowledge and skills to help the learner grow.

When we think of the different types of relationships, we begin to see that each relationship plays an important role in our lives. Keep in mind that each relationship contributes to our lives differently, and no relationship is more important than the other. They all work together to create a balanced and meaningful life.

Now that we understand the importance of our relationships, we can take a look at the evolution of our social relationships over time. Come with us as we explore the evolution of our relationships in modern society.

The Evolution of Social Interaction in Modern Society

To understand the impact of technology on social interaction and communication, we need to take a brief look into the history of communication and how it has changed as human beings have evolved.

A Brief Look Into the History of Communication

Language, both written and spoken, has taken thousands of years to develop and perfect. With that being said, many point to hieroglyphics as the first point of reference for written communication. Although we aren't wrong, even before this, rock paintings and hand and smoke signals were primarily used during primitive times. Rock paintings, smoke, and hand signals were used to mark territory or communicate information with other tribes. It wasn't until 3000 B.C.E. that we started using hieroglyphics and cuneiform to record information on papyrus or clay tablets. This form of writing became a major breakthrough in our ability to communicate with others without the use of verbal language.

In 6 B.C.E., we saw another improvement in our ability to communicate as our first postal system came into existence through the Persian Empire. The system operated through a network of messengers who delivered messages from one city to another, enabling communication between cities and people. From this point on, upgrades in communication wouldn't be seen in the Western world until the 15th century with the invention of the printing press by Johannes Gutenberg, though China had already started the printing process in the year 700.

The printing press revolutionized communication by offering us the chance to communicate with others on a wider scale. This is because we could now print newspapers, books, pamphlets, and more and share them with the masses. Unknowingly to Johannes, this laid the foundation for mass media and communication.

Before the telephone, there was the telegraph, which was developed in 1837 by Samuel Morse. The telegraph used a system of dots and dashes known as Morse code that could be transmitted through telegraph wires. This invention could be used for long-distance communication, making the task of communicating easier. However, this breakthrough wouldn't last for long, as less than 40 years later, we saw the invention of the telephone.

The invention of the telephone in 1876 by Alexander Graham Bell took the world by storm and changed the trajectory of communication forever by offering us the opportunity to communicate verbally no matter where we were. This invention laid the foundation for the modern smartphones of today, which make communicating and finding information simple and easy. From this point on, we have inventions like the television, radio, email, and internet, all of which took place in the 20th century. The creation of the internet birthed what we know as modern society and communication, with social media platforms taking the lead to make communication and keeping in touch easier.

The Impact of Technology on Social Behavior

Technology has influenced various aspects of our lives, altering our behavior over time. In this section, we explore how technology has altered our social behavior.

To define social behavior, we first need to start by defining behavior. Both behavior and social behavior mean the same thing and can be defined as how we conduct ourselves in the presence of others. Usually, social behaviors affect the individuals we interact with and may have a positive or negative effect on those people.

In the early 1980s, a report was issued by the National Science Foundation with regard to its forecast on technology and the implications it may have on families, businesses, politics, and the American population as a whole. Although their forecasts and findings were centered around America, the world at large would be on the receiving end of these findings and forecasts. The report stated that technology would transform and revolutionize our families, businesses, and political organizations. Even though these reports were made in the early 1980s, they couldn't have hit the nail more on the head. With the ushering in of the golden age of technology came a few changes, including some in our human behavior.

One of the many inventions that has contributed to our decline in social interaction is the smartphone. Our smartphones have become exceptionally immersive, with creators coming up with new features daily. In fact, these days, we no longer have to look any further than our smartphones for things like food, monetary transactions, entertainment, and more. Our smartphones can connect to almost anything, including our homes. Although this may seem convenient, it comes with its fair share of problems.

Increased smartphone usage has been linked to things like lower empathy levels in both children and adults. Not only are we losing our empathy, but we're also losing our overall satisfaction with life itself. This is due to our constant exposure to the social media lives and achievements of others.

The more we focus on our smartphones, the more we become desensitized to our feelings and ability to function normally as human beings. This in turn fosters antisocial behaviors, which can, and in many cases does, lead to antisocial behaviors and eventual isolation.

Our smartphones can also lead to a decrease in productivity. This is because everything, both necessary and unnecessary, is at our fingertips. Apps such as TikTok, Instagram, Facebook, and more are created to captivate our attention and leave us constantly looking at our smartphones. This leaves us constantly distracted, which can lead to lower levels of concentration, which affects our ability to be productive. More people have been diagnosed with ADHD and the scattered-brain phenomenon due to a decrease in concentration.

Outside of these alarming implications of smartphones and technology, there has also been a decrease in IQ levels, shorter concentration spans, and an increase in phone addictions. These have been linked to issues with problem-solving skills, which are needed for daily human survival.

Changes in Societal Norms and Their Effects on Relationships

One of the many things technology has afforded us is ease and convenience. It does this by changing how we usually do things and offering us simpler, faster, and sometimes more cost-effective ways of operating. In fact, technological advancements have revolutionized almost every industry, including engineering, medicine, agriculture, mining, and more.

In 2020, we saw the height of what technology can do as businesses and other industries sought different ways to keep their businesses afloat. With hard lockdown restrictions, multiple businesses had to find their way around new operations, with technology coming to the rescue. In fact, during this time, multiple business owners discovered that they were still able to make money even though their physical locations were closed. This is because they still had outlets, such as social media, online stores, and more, to assist them in making the money they needed.

During this time, multiple businesses used applications such as Google Meet, Microsoft Teams, Zoom, and more to keep in touch and conduct meetings. Thanks to technology, business operations could be conducted, children could still attend lessons, groceries could be delivered, and people could still keep in touch.

However, when we flip the coin, we begin to see another side of technology and its impact.

In the last 500 years, technological advancements have left many without jobs or means to feed their families. This is due to the automation of some jobs, as businesses were trying to save on costs and become more efficient. A prime example of this can be seen in the agricultural industry, where there have been multiple technological improvements to assist with the demand for food and meat. To keep the cost of growing food low, farmers have had to look into more affordable ways of growing food and looking after animals. When prices were compared, the automated one-time purchase seemed like the best way to go instead of paying monthly salaries or hiring temporary staff.

The same can be said for businesses and marketing. Technology has opened up various doors with marketing, affording businesses the chance to engage with their customers on their favorite social media platforms with their favorite social media influencer. Although this may sound amazing, there are two main issues with this type of marketing business model. The first is that it takes away from the buyer's experience, and the second is that it can increase our purchasing habits.

Taking Away From the Buyer Experience

Purchasing a product is more than just taking it home. While making these purchases, we do things like walk around and ask for assistance, therefore interacting with others and more. The purchasing experience offers us the chance to interact with others, get fresh air, walk around, and clear our minds.

Technology takes this experience away and replaces it with an online purchasing experience that only requires you to have a stable internet connection, a smart device, and money. The process of delivery is far worse, as many of us do not even interact with our delivery personnel but rather prefer that they drop the package at our door and leave.

Increase in Purchasing Habits

Scrolling through social media can show you what you do and don't have. With social media influencers showcasing new products or services every day, it can get a little tempting to make that purchase even if you don't need the product or service. In fact, studies show that around 8% to 16% of the general public may suffer from compulsive shopping disorder.

Due to the increase in online purchases, online stores have done their best to ensure that buyers are getting value for money by offering incentives. Buyers may find themselves being offered discounts, free delivery, points, recommendations, and more. The point is to ensure that buyers feel rewarded for making online purchases, thus keeping them in the cycle of continuously wanting to buy something new.

The dangers of compulsive shopping disorder include issues with finances, an increased risk of anxiety and depression, and overall issues with livelihood and hoarding.

Technology has changed societal norms and has forced many of us to adopt new behaviors. Unfortunately for us, we're still trying to navigate through the maze known as technology, meaning that we're going to make mistakes, which can cost us greatly. Finding a balance between technology and normal life can become a challenge because of how dependent many of us have become.

Many of us are finding that our real-life relationships are falling apart because we're unable to connect without technology in the mix. We find ourselves struggling to create real connections that lead to promising relationships. Instead, many of us are being exposed to false information about what healthy relationships look like. In the end, we find ourselves in toxic and unhealthy relationships because we're seeking to belong. Not only does this harm our perspective on relationships and keep us in toxic thought patterns, it also leads us to think poorly of ourselves, thus creating a poor self-image.

Defining Good Social Relationships

Part of building social relationships is understanding what good and healthy social relationships are while finding the balance between giving and receiving. In this section, we take a deeper look into social relationships by defining what a good and healthy relationship looks like and what it means to give and receive.

Characteristics of Healthy and Productive Relationships

Healthy and productive relationships have certain characteristics associated with them. In this section, we explore the characteristics of a healthy and productive relationship.

Respect

Respect can be defined as showing regard or consideration toward the abilities, worth, views, opinions, and more of others. Getting into social relationships means respecting and considering the feelings and emotions of the other party, even after being with that person for an extended period of time.

Vulnerability

Emotional vulnerability can be described as our willingness to address and articulate our emotions. When we're vulnerable, we're allowing others in and affording them the chance to be a part of what we're going through. To be emotionally vulnerable, you must be self-aware and have the ability to acknowledge and deal with emotions in ways that do not harm others.

Trust

Emotional vulnerability cannot function without trust. When we can trust our partners, we afford ourselves the luxury of vulnerability, even in the midst of a breach of trust. Building and sustaining trust takes time, which is why you'll always want to ensure that you build trust slowly while also ensuring that you're going at a healthy pace.

Honesty

Lies breed barriers that leave us unable to express ourselves in a manner that fosters a healthy relationship. When we're honest, no matter how ugly the truth may be, we build a healthy and solid relationship and foundation. Anything built on a lie will not be healthy and safe in the long run.

Empathy

Empathy is our ability to place ourselves in the shoes of others to understand and share their feelings. We may not be able to fix their problems; however, creating space for them to express their emotions can be of great assistance. It fosters an environment that allows both you and others to share your feelings without fear of judgment.

Kindness

A key characteristic of a healthy and productive relationship is kindness. When we're kind, we have the ability to be considerate and thoughtful toward the people we engage with. By thinking about and understanding your partner's needs, you can assist them where necessary.

Boundaries

A healthy and productive relationship consists of boundaries. Boundaries can be seen as the parameters we are willing to work with or within. They outline how far we are willing to go and what we are comfortable with. Every individual should have their own boundaries that need to be communicated in a healthy manner. When our boundaries are communicated and followed, we find ourselves feeling safe, seen, trusted, and valued, which can help us have a positive outlook on our relationships. Boundaries can come in the form of emotional, physical, spiritual, or even financial boundaries.

Commitment

Maintaining and building healthy relationships is tough, especially when you're juggling other aspects of life. By remaining committed to the relationship, no matter what that relationship may be, you put in the work to keep it productive and healthy. In layman's terms, something only works when you make it work; hence, it needs to be backed up by commitment.

Forgiveness

Getting into a relationship with someone means creating an opportunity for you to experience disappointment. Disappointment can show up as multiple things for different people; however, it isn't the disappointment that may be the issue but rather our ability or inability to forgive. When we are unable to forgive, we can hold on to bitterness, anger, and hurt, which can show up as constant bickering. Fighting consistently can lead to a breakdown of trust and emotional safety, which can cause the relationship to turn toxic and then fail.

Appreciation and Validation

Appreciation and validation are forms of gratitude and acknowledgement. They ensure that those we engage with know that their presence is valued and that their feelings, opinions, and views are taken into consideration.

Healthy and productive relationships are built over an extended period of time. By identifying whether your relationships are healthy and productive, you afford yourself the chance to walk away from any relationships that are either toxic or do not fulfill you as an individual.

Now that we understand the characteristics of a healthy and happy relationship, we can look into balancing the power dynamic of giving and receiving.

The Balance Between Giving and Receiving in Relationships

Part of defining good social relationships is looking into the power dynamic of giving and receiving. For many of us, we are caught in relationships that require too much of us or are stuck in toxic thinking patterns that leave us unable to receive. In this section, we explore the idea of giving and receiving while looking at how we can balance the two.

The concept of giving and receiving plays an integral part in any relationship. When we think of this concept, many of us tend to think of a give-and-take situation, which requires a balance between giving and receiving. Our relationship with giving and receiving can, and in many cases is, affected by our perception of ourselves as well as the environment and our past traumas or lack thereof. This could mean different things for different people; however, general cases suggest that many are uncomfortable with the idea of receiving while others are simply willing to receive and not give.

By creating a balance between giving and receiving, you avoid the issues that arise when there is an imbalance between the two. These issues may include anger, resentment, feelings of being emotionally drained, and more. Keep in mind that giving and receiving go far beyond monetary exchange and are usually associated with emotional needs such as support, affection, and general emotional presence in the relationship.

Bringing a balance between giving and receiving can prove to be difficult, especially when you're just starting out. To improve the giving and receiving dynamic in your relationships, you can:

Start With Understanding the Importance of Giving and Receiving

For us to create a balance between giving and receiving, we first need to understand its importance and purpose. Why are we seeking balance, and what does that look like to us? Are we givers or receivers, and what in our past has made us this way? Is there room for change within our giving and receiving dynamic? Are you being completely honest with yourself about the role you play in this relationship when it comes to giving and receiving?

Many times, we tend to think that simply understanding what it means to give and receive is enough; however, there is a certain depth to understanding the role we play in our own relationships. By answering these questions honestly, we are able to build an appropriate picture of what the basics of our relationship with giving and receiving are. From this point, we can move forward, understanding that we too contribute toward the giving and receiving dynamic of our relationships.

Outline Your Needs and the Boundaries You May Need

As human beings, we are wired to have needs. To successfully balance the give-and-take dynamic, we need to ensure that we know what our needs are and the boundaries we need to put in place to maintain our dynamic. The questions asked in the previous paragraph should help you outline what it is you need from those you engage with while affording you the chance to evaluate who you are in your relationships and the reasons behind your feelings.

Exercise Compassion

The journey to change is filled with many mistakes, so you'll need to be compassionate not only toward yourself but to other parties involved in your change. Doing so can afford both you and those around you the grace to change.

Communicate and Start Small

The hardest part of change is starting, which is why starting small can make a major difference. When starting, you'll always want to keep in mind that small steps are still steps and that changing anything is a major undertaking. Making changes, even in small increments, requires that we be honest with those around us, meaning that we'll need to communicate our changes. When communicating these changes, you'll want to be assertive and not aggressive. Communicating boundaries can cause the other party to feel as though they are not doing enough, and no matter how true this may be, you'll want to ensure that you're calm. Remaining calm will afford you the chance to think clearly while also maintaining a non-threatening demeanor.

Finding balance can be hard, especially when you're looking to do something for the first time. Although change is scary, it is also necessary to maintain healthy and productive relationships. In the next chapter, we explore the foundations of healthy social relationships.

THE FOUNDATIONS OF SOCIAL RELATIONSHIPS

Knowing others is intelligence; knowing yourself is true wisdom. –Lao Tzu

Foundation: the groundwork or basics of anything that needs to be built whether physical, emotional, spiritual, financial, or psychological. Without the proper foundation, whatever we're building cannot and will not last. The same can be said for building and maintaining healthy social relationships. In this chapter, we take a look at the foundations of social relationships.

Understanding Self

Oftentimes, when seeking to create authentic and healthy social relationships, we abandon our self in order to create and sustain healthy social relationships. When creating authentic and healthy relationships, you'll want to ensure that you understand your sense of self.

Self-Discovery: The Journey

Self-discovery is an ongoing journey that requires us to look within and recognize our self-worth. Self-worth is our ability to see ourselves as deserving of love, affection, belonging, and more from others. Many tend to use self-esteem and self-worth interchangeably and, although they seem similar, they are not the same. Self-esteem is more focused on our capability to trust our strengths, capabilities, and worth. When we think of self-esteem, we need to think of our self-belief and our emotional states, which can be despair, shame, joy, and more. To start the journey of self-discovery, we can:

1. Understand the importance of your self-worth. By knowing our self-worth, we will have the confidence to maneuver set boundaries and demand respect. We also afford ourselves the chance to recognize when we are being treated poorly and have the understanding that this is not a fault on our

part. When we acknowledge our value, we're able to let go of self-doubt and embrace that we are worthy of love, respect, happiness, and affection.
2. Let go of societal expectations of what you should be and embrace who you are. By shedding these layers, we also let go of any self-criticism that may be pushing us to accept the things we do not deserve.
3. Avoid people-pleasing, which has become an issue for many of us. People pleasing is when we are constantly looking to feel valued and appreciated, thus abandoning our own needs to fulfill the needs of others. This can be detrimental as it keeps us in toxic mindsets and environments that can hinder our journey and harm us on a mental and emotional level.

Keep in mind that growth is a journey and, although there have been many on this path, the experience and journey will be different for all who decided to embark on it. Below we offer a blueprint that assist you on your journey to self-discovery.

1. Start by visualizing your ideal self and the lifestyle associated with this change. The idea is to have a point of reference: something you're working towards to help make the process a lot easier. When you know where you're going it's easier to make the right decisions.
2. Take stock of your passions, interests, and dreams. Our dreams, passions, and interests are one of the best ways to get intimate with ourselves. When we neglect ourselves for extended periods, we lose a sense of who we are; however, going back to our interests, passions, and dreams can help to ignite what we've left dormant for so long.
3. When we're comfortable, we stop the process of growth and trying new things. Trying new things can help us discover different layers of ourselves and help shift us toward something we might be interested in. Seeing new

things can help revitalize our inner beings and give us the push we need to move forward.
4. The journey to self-discovery also lies in our ability to consider our skills. Being good at something can help with our self-image. When we know what we're good at, we're able to admire ourselves.
5. Journaling is an amazing way to keep track of our thoughts, experiences, and life changes. The more we journal, the more we keep track of our lives and the easier it becomes to discover new things about ourselves.
6. When seeking change, one of the best things we can do for ourselves is seek outside assistance. This means doing things such as reading books, listening to a podcast, watching a YouTube video on personal growth and development, or even contracting the services of a life coach or mentor. This step is simply about finding a way to get to your desired goal and having the information you need to get there.
7. Build mental and emotional stamina. Recovering from unhealthy habits can be daunting, especially when you're still in the same thought patterns or cycles. Building mental and emotional stamina can assist in ensuring that you stay on track and safeguard you from the opinions and thoughts of others.

Understanding self can seem tedious; however, it is worth it, especially when you're looking to build and maintain healthy relationships. Along the way, you may discover toxic thought patterns or need to heal from certain situations that enforced and created toxic thought patterns. Remember that you are worthy of gentleness, kindness, and compassion.

The Role of Self-Esteem in Forming and Maintaining Relationships

In the previous section, we defined self-esteem; however, in this section, we take an in-depth look at the role self-esteem plays in forming and maintaining social relationships.

The Link Between Self-Esteem and Relationship Satisfaction

Our self-esteem can have a profound effect on the relationships we decide to foster and maintain. This is because our self-esteem can affect how we're able to receive love, affection, and care. When this happens, it can affect our level of satisfaction with the relationship. People with lower self-esteem levels have been shown to have satisfaction issues with their relationships. Although satisfaction within every relationship tends to change over time, people with higher self-esteem have been shown to maintain, if not slightly lower their levels of satisfaction within a relationship.

How Self-Esteem Affects Our Relationships

Our childhood plays a major role in our ability to function in relationships. When we're neglected as children, we may develop unhealthy habits as adults. For example, when we come from dysfunctional families, we're more likely not to have a voice. This means that we continue to accept poor treatment because we believe we are not worthy of being treated well. Usually, these traits are passed down from one generation to another, meaning that our parents were exposed to similar behavior, thus they display it. These toxic mindsets can come in the form of abuse, a lack of communication or poor communication skills, a lack of boundaries, aggression, emotional neglect, an inability to cooperate, and more. This can cause us to become anxious, insecure, angry, cannot trust others, have low self-esteem, or become emotionally withdrawn.

Attachment Styles

Emotional neglect can cause us to develop something called an attachment style. An attachment style can be described as the way we relate to others, especially in intimate relationships. Our attachment style is influenced by our self-worth, interpersonal trust, and how well or poorly we bonded with others as children.

Our attachment styles can and have been linked to our self-esteem. Although there are various attachment styles, in this section, we will be focusing on the anxious and avoidant attachment styles. Keep in mind that these are two extremes meaning that they both lie on opposite ends. One is consistently pursuing while the other is consistently avoiding. The one in pursuit will most likely struggle to be alone while the one who is avoiding will struggle or avoid being too close.

An anxious attachment style will continuously have you in the loop of being fixated on your relationship to the point of abandoning your own needs. Usually, your sole intention is to please and accommodate your partner. Although you may derive pleasure from your partner being happy, you will ultimately feel that your needs are not being met hence your dissatisfaction. Additionally, you may take things personally causing you to see those you are in a relationship with negatively. Due to issues with your self-esteem, you may find yourself unable to speak up about the issues in the relationship causing a lack or loss of intimacy. You may also find yourself becoming jealous of those your partner gives attention to. Ultimately, this behavior will lead to both parties being unhappy and therefore an inability to move forward in the relationship.

On the other hand, having an avoidant attachment style means that you intentionally avoid closeness and or intimacy. You do this by using distancing behaviors which include addiction, ignoring the needs of your partner, dismissing their feelings, and more. The point is to avoid all forms of closeness while remaining hyper-vigilant to any forms of control or limitations placed on you. Unfortunately, these behaviors will push partners away causing feelings of unhappiness and dissatisfaction which will ultimately cause the relationship to fall apart.

Communication and Self-Esteem

When we think of self-esteem, rarely are we ever thinking about our ability to communicate. Being in a relationship with anyone requires that we communicate our feelings, thoughts, trauma, needs, and more. Growing up in a dysfunctional home means that we were witness to unhealthy communication methods that we later adopt or deny. Generally, when we are codependent, we struggle with articulating our feelings, wants, and needs because we were either shamed or ignored during our childhood when doing so. As adults, this will cause us to suppress or outright deny our feelings due to us not wanting to feel the same way again or not wanting to face the criticism or emotional abandonment that comes with doing so. Instead, we tend to rely on other tactics such as mind reading, asking questions, blaming, lying, avoiding the problem or problems, caretaking, and even controlling or ignoring our partner as a whole.

Good communication requires that we speak clearly, are honest, concise, assertive, listen well, and have the ability to communicate our needs, wants, feelings, and boundaries. Unfortunately, because of the issues that stem from our childhoods, we may find this difficult and foreign, which can and will affect the stability of the relationship.

Boundaries and Self-Esteem

One of the many things we may find ourselves struggling with is setting boundaries. This can be attributed to coming from a dysfunctional family where healthy boundaries were never practiced. Instead, as children, some were made to be controlled, disrespected, and used for the needs of their parents, which either killed or undermined their self-esteem. This leads to them struggling to accept the boundaries, differences, or space requests of others.

Boundaries are meant to protect us and afford us the ability to say no. When we struggle with boundaries, we tend to take what others say personally and may feel responsible for the emotions of others. This will cause conflict and make our partners feel as though they are unable to express themselves without offending. The more this behavior continues, the more the relationship becomes unstable, and over time the relationship will end.

Our self-esteem plays a major role in our ability to function well in relationships. To build a healthy and functioning relationship, we'll need to adjust our mindset and work on our self-esteem and past trauma.

Overcoming Personal Barriers to Build Better Relationships

In the previous section, we saw the potential impact that our childhood can have on our relationships and our ability to function in them. In this section, we take a look at how we can overcome personal barriers to help us build better relationships.

Personal Barriers Defined

A boundary is defined as a line that marks a limit of an area. Personal boundaries can be described as something similar; however, this is from a personal level. This means that a personal barrier is a limitation in what we can or cannot do. For many of us, when we think of a personal barrier, we're also thinking about a personal boundary. Usually, a personal boundary is associated with personal growth and development, affording us the chance to fill our cups. Personal barriers, on the other hand, are usually centered around limitations instead of capabilities. This leads us to question whether all personal barriers are bad.

When trying to define whether a personal barrier is bad, you'll want to question whether it promotes or hinders growth. There are several examples we could give about personal barriers that are meant to protect us. For example, let's say you've recently experienced a home invasion or have been assaulted by a stranger. Your first instinct would be to install cameras in your home or upgrade your security system. With being assaulted by a stranger, your first instinct is to be wary of any and almost all strangers. These personal barriers are usually implemented due to previous trauma. They are a defense mechanism used to help us protect ourselves from experiencing something similar.

Overcoming Personal Barriers

Personal barriers are a result of past trauma that was inflicted. This means that many of our barriers are unhealthy or do not assist us with personal growth, and development and can hinder our ability to create thriving relationships. For this reason, we must overcome unhealthy personal barriers to create and sustain healthy and productive relationships.

Personal Barriers With Communication

Personal barriers come in different forms, with one of the biggest being communication. When we communicate, it's always important to understand that we are not simply conveying a message, we're conveying a message we'd like to be understood. Being poor communicators can hinder us from fully being able to express ourselves or express ourselves in a manner that allows us to be heard and understood.

Keep in mind that any personal barrier is unique to our own experience as human beings. This means that our ability or inability to communicate is shaped by our emotions, perceptions, traumatic experiences, and more. Our cultural background may also play a major role in our ability to function as adults. Some cultures may value silence more than they do personal relationships and growth. Whatever the reason for communication issues, it is our responsibility to fix our issues with communication.

To fix our barriers, we need to understand them. In this section, we tackle a few components that may be affecting our ability to communicate.

Anxiety and Fear

When we're fearful and anxious, we rarely can express ourselves in a manner that everyone can understand. Instead, fear and anxiety can cause us to hesitate when sharing our thoughts and opinions due to fear of rejection or judgment from others.

When trying to overcome fear and anxiety, it is imperative that we build our communication skills. One way of achieving this is by being an active listener meaning that we afford others the chance to express their views and opinions while processing what they're saying. Practicing active listening will also afford us the chance to express our views. You can also practice positive self-talk while seeking feedback from a few trusted individuals. This can help us learn to express ourselves better while also boosting our self-confidence.

A Lack of Self-Awareness

Self-awareness can play a major role in our personal barriers. When we're unaware of ourselves it leads to constant misunderstandings due to interpretation issues. Being self-aware means that we can take stock of our emotions, feelings, intentions, and communication styles. By being aware of these we ensure that we are not sending mixed signals and that others are interpreting our messages correctly.

When trying to improve self-awareness you can make simple adjustments such as journaling, understanding your own emotions and communication style, asking for feedback from others, and putting down our defenses to make us more approachable.

Stereotypes and Judgments

When we're wounded, we tend to come up with preconceived ideas of what we believe people are and the character that is associated with them. We do this to protect ourselves from the unknown variable of their character. During this process, we may come up with stereotypical judgments that may hinder our ability to communicate with them.

To combat these barriers, we need to embark on the journey of healing and self-discovery. What about them causes us to pass judgment? Which part of us is unhealed therefore blurring the line between what they're saying and what we're hearing?

Issues with communication in personal barriers spill over to almost all aspects of our lives. When we begin the process of healing, we step into who we truly are, thus leading us to blossom. By redefining our personal barriers and boundaries, we can overcome the issues that lie at the heart of why we become the way we are.

Communication Skills

As people, our ability to communicate plays a major role in our ability to function in relationships. In this book, we have touched on communication briefly; however, in this section, we take a deeper look into communication and the skills required to become an effective communicator.

The Art of Communication: Techniques for Effective Communication

When we think of communication, the last thing we're thinking about is art. Art is a form of expression or the application of human creativity and imagination and can also be described as various forms of creativity. Communication can be seen as a form of art because it allows us to express ourselves and be creative. It offers us the opportunity to express our ideas, thoughts, imagination, or even creativity within certain spaces, which makes communication an art.

The art of communication is simply the transmission of information from one person to the next. The idea is to convey a specific message while ensuring that the receiver fully understands the content of the message. The art of communication can always be learned, unlearned, and relearned as long as we are trying to better ourselves and our way of communicating.

There are five main types of communication, which include:

Verbal Communication

Verbal communication occurs when we speak or engage in conversation with others. This can be any form of communication where there is a verbal exchange between two or more people. For example, having a Zoom call can be considered verbal communication.

We can have formal or informal forms of verbal communication. Formal communication is usually associated with a meeting, conference, speech, or more. Informal communication is when we sit down with a friend over coffee to discuss our problems. Either way, the communication is happening, and it's being done in a manner that can be considered verbal.

Non-Verbal Communication

Non-verbal communication, also known as non-verbal cues, is simply our body language during conversation. When we speak, we're not only speaking with our words, but we're also communicating a message with our body language. When communicating, you'll want to ensure that your body language is in line with the message you're trying to convey. Non-verbal cues include things such as eye contact, posture, facial expressions, movement, and touch.

Written Communication

One of the most common forms of communication is written communication. This category includes all forms of written communication including emails, social media posts, blogs, and more.

In today's age, where the internet is something we use regularly, it's vital to understand that what we write and send can affect or follow us for life. Always write something you'd always be happy to be associated with.

Active Listening

Usually, this type of communication doesn't make it into any list; however, to communicate well, we are meant to listen with Intention. Active listening or listening with Intention is simply about allowing the person we are engaging with a chance to speak. When we allow others to speak, we free ourselves from the expectation that we must have all the answers.

Visual Communication

In today's age, visual communication is at an all-time high, especially with social media platforms. Visual communication is the ability for us to communicate an idea in the form of a picture or video. We see these today more than ever through memes, ads on social media platforms, billboards, and other forms of communication.

By understanding the different types of communication, we're able to ensure that we're communicating effectively. Keep in mind that everything in today's world is happening through social media. This may cause many to either disregard or completely abandon other forms of communication.

Reading and Expressing Non-Verbal Cues

In the previous section, we took a brief look at non-verbal cues. In this section, we take a deeper look into non-verbal cues and how you can read and express them.

While we're communicating, our bodies tend to send off signals that have a lot to do with demeanor and facial expressions. Usually, these signals allude to how we truly feel about a certain situation, person, or event. These gestures can be considered as non-verbal cues and contribute majorly toward how a certain situation is perceived. Our non-verbal communication can build trust, put people at ease, or draw people closer; however, it can also break trust, push people away, and cause confusion.

Reading and Expressing

In the previous section, we expressed how communication is a form of art and that we can learn, unlearn, and relearn how we communicate. By improving and understanding non-verbal cues, we're able to communicate better. So what is the importance of non-verbal cues and what role do they play?

Have you ever had a conversation and left feeling as though the person you spoke to cared? Can you think back to what made you believe that they cared? Was it the way they looked at you or how they constantly kept eye contact as you explained your side of the story?

Non-verbal cues are more than just how our bodies respond to certain situations. They are elements of conversation that show our true intentions. When our cues align with our words it assists in building and maintaining our relationships.

Improving Non-Verbal Cues

One of the many things we tend to miss during conversation is non-verbal cues. If we're constantly distracted, thinking about something else, or under immense pressure, causing us to be anxious and worried, we may miss non-verbal cues or risk giving off negative non-verbal cues. In this section, we take a look at how you can improve your non-verbal cues to help with effective communication.

Learn to Manage Stress and Anxiety

Emotions can be just as contagious as the flu. When we're stressed or anxious, we may send off-putting non-verbal cues, leaving those that we're communicating with confused or upset. This can negatively impact already stressful situations and cause those involved to not want to engage in conversation with us.

When feeling stressed or overwhelmed, it's always best to take a minute to breathe and gather our thoughts and emotions. During this time, you can take a moment to meditate, use a squeeze ball, or go through the five senses grounding technique. This technique requires that we use our senses to help shift the focus from the stressful situation to our present moment which can help us let go of stress and anxiety.

Develop Emotional Awareness

Emotional awareness, also known as emotional intelligence, is the ability to use, perceive, manage, understand, and or handle our own or others' emotions. During conversations, we can be easily ruled by our emotions, causing us to overreact or say or do things that we'll later come to regret.

Being emotionally aware affords us the chance to accurately read other people's non-verbal cues and builds trust while also showing others that we care about them and their emotional needs.

For many of us, dealing with our feelings or emotions is something we try to suppress. Even though we may be successful in suppressing our emotions, we still run the risk of our emotions affecting us. By developing our emotional awareness, we're able to gain control over our behavior and deal with emotions as effectively as possible.

Reading Body Language

When we're able to regulate and read our own emotions, it becomes easier for us to do the same with others. You can accurately read body language by:

- Paying Attention to Inconsistencies

Verbal and non-verbal communication work together to send out the same message. When our body language differs from our verbal communication, it is considered an inconsistency. By paying attention to these inconsistencies, we're able to get information and find out if what's being communicated is what is being communicated is true.

When trying to decipher non-verbal communication, you'll always want to look at things holistically instead of isolating a singular incident. This means that instead of looking at one gesture, you'll need to look at all gestures to come up with a solid conclusion.

- Trust Your Instinct

Oftentimes, we're discouraged from trusting our instincts; however, these feelings can help in finding the true meaning behind messages. When doing this, you'll want to use your knowledge of non-verbal cues as well as your judgment.

The Importance of Empathy in Understanding

> *Empathy is seeing with the eyes of another, listening with the ears of another, and feeling with the heart of another.* –Alfred Adler

In today's world of technology, the ability to see into the lives of others has become a norm. We even have the ability to chime in via comment sections of social media posts. We're constantly looking and watching the lives of others. You'd think that this would make us more empathetic; however, the case is the reverse.

Empathy Defined

Empathy can be described as our ability to understand and share the feelings of others. This means that we're able to place ourselves in their shoes and understand their feelings and frustrations toward a certain situation or person. Our ability or inability to be empathetic greatly affects our social relationships while also affecting people's perceptions of who we are. This is because empathetic people are usually caring, warm, and nurturing while those who lack empathy can be seen as cold, self-absorbed, and self-centered.

In recent times, people have taken an interest in empathy and its ability to affect relationships. It was found that there are three kinds of empathy which include:

Cognitive Empathy

Cognitive empathy relies on our ability to understand and identify other people's emotions. This means that although we're able to put ourselves in someone else's shoes, we do not sense or feel the emotions associated with what they're going through.

Emotional Empathy

Emotional empathy, also known as emotional contagion, is when we can feel what the other person is going through on both an emotional and physical level. This type of empathy would be best suited for those who are in the medical or healthcare profession.

Compassionate Empathy

When we have compassionate empathy, we're able to not only understand and feel what someone else is feeling, but we use our feelings, emotions, and understanding to assist them. Due to our ability to understand their situation intimately we're able to provide them with the support they need.

All forms of empathy are important and can play vital roles in different situations. Empathy, in all its forms, has its advantages which include:

- Our ability to be empathetic can have a profound effect on our social relationships. It helps us to understand the feelings of those we are in relationship with meaning that we're able to offer adequate support.
- To build social connections, we need to have empathy to feel as connected as possible to those we engage with. Forming these types of connections can help us feel valued, loved, and cared for. This can help us with overall well-being as it can increase our feelings of self-worth and happiness.
- When we're empathetic, we're also able to anticipate the needs of others. This means that we can offer adequate support.
- Being empathetic can boost our leadership skills, as it affords us the chance to communicate well with others not only as individuals but in a group setting.

Empathy can play a major role in how we're perceived and our overall well-being. By being empathetic, we not only save ourselves but others as well.

Handling Difficult Conversation

Being in social relationships means that we are constantly engaging with others. While doing this, we may find that there is conflict within the spaces we hold. By knowing and understanding how to handle difficult conversations, we can avoid major arguments and create and maintain peace.

Difficult Conversations Defined

A difficult conversation is a planned discussion that is centered around an unpleasant experience or uncomfortable topic. The goal of having difficult conversations is to share different perspectives while building mutual respect. The idea is to share each other's perspective not to persuade or try to win the disagreement. When we avoid these types of conversations, we can create space for feelings of resentment and stress, while also leaving room for the issue to be escalated.

Although difficult conversations are hard to have, there are a few benefits to having them, including:

- coming up with a resolution that works well for everyone involved
- opportunity to repair the relationship
- embracing constructive criticism and change
- gaining a deeper understanding of the issue at hand

Our ability to handle difficult conversations is vital, especially when we plan on saving those relationships. Now that we have a concrete understanding of what difficult conversations are, we can move on to how we can handle them.

How to Handle Difficult Conversations

Handling difficult conversations doesn't come easy to everyone. Thankfully, the art of handling difficult conversations is something that can be learned. In this section, we cover how to handle difficult conversations.

1. *Have the Conversation Early*

Prolonging difficult conversations can lead to anxiety and stress while also raising the stakes for the conversation. For this reason, you'll want to engage in this type of conversation as soon as possible.

When we face difficult conversations early, we spare ourselves the complexity of that conflict spilling over into other relationships or conversations. We also afford ourselves justification for having the conversation.

2. *Think of Your Set Goals for the Conversation*

Having a difficult conversation that addresses all conflicts is hard, especially when tempers arise. Amid the conversation, we can forget important points and things we'd like to address. By coming up with set goals and points, we can combat this issue and ensure that all points of interest are addressed. Also, writing down our points of concern and goals can assist us in guiding the conversation to a resolution.

3. *Choose Your Location Wisely*

Playing on even ground during the process of conflict resolution is vital. You'll want to ensure that you pick an appropriate environment to have your conversation. This means looking into finding neutral ground and assessing whether all parties involved will be comfortable with the location. Depending on the topic, you may want to choose a public space to ensure that people's emotions remain in check.

4. *Come With an Open Mind and Listen*

One of the many things we can do during conflict resolution is to listen with the intention of understanding. This means showing up with an open mind that's ready to engage from an objective point of view.

When we show up with this type of mindset, we afford the other parties a chance to explain their side of the story along with their perspective.

5. *Empathy*

In this chapter, we covered the importance of empathy in social relationships; however, empathy is just as important in conflict resolution. When we have empathy, we're able to put ourselves in other people's shoes and see things from their perspective. We're also able to reassure the other party that we are solely here for conflict resolution rather than proving that we are correct.

6. *Have a Conflict Resolution Mindset*

Tackle conflict with the idea of conflict resolution. This means that we come up with a solution that we think is best. Coming up with this solution means that we stay on course for the conversation. Make sure to bring up your resolution while also leaving room for others to state their solutions.

In this case, you'll want to ensure that you're affording others the chance to speak and bring up their issues and potential solutions.

7. *Use First Person*

During arguments, we may find ourselves using language that attacks the person we're arguing with. By using first person, you instantly become non-threatening and explain the issue from your perspective.

8. *Implore REM Strategies*

Imploring REM strategies simply means that we focus on relevant facts rather than discussing things from a personal perspective. When we use these strategies, we're able to take accountability for our part and identify what the problem was while also discussing the impact of the problem. Doing this can help other parties to not feel attacked.

9. *Practice Active Listening and Ask Questions*

Usually when we're mediating and trying to resolve conflict, we come with preconceived ideas of what truly happened. This can hinder our ability to hear the other side of the story. By asking questions and practicing active listening, we're able to hear the other side of the story.

10. *Manage Emotions*

Conflict is usually attached to emotion. When trying to deal with conflict you may experience emotions such as anger, hurt, disbelief, and more; however, we must learn to manage our emotions during this time. Always ensure that your emotions do not get the best of you to maintain order within the conflict resolution discussions. While doing this, you may want to check on the emotional state of the other party and do your best to keep them as calm and collected as possible.

11. *Show Confidence*

Before handling conflict, you'll always want to think of your side of the story and how certain things made you feel. This will afford you the chance to speak with confidence and let the other party know that you've thought about your story and how the situation affected you. This can be of great assistance when the other party may try to discredit your version of events.

12. *Take a Break*

If you've ever dealt with conflict, then you'll know how difficult it is to handle, especially when emotions are involved. Things tend to become heated, leaving both parties or one in an emotional state. When you feel this coming on, it's always best to take a break to gather yourself and your thoughts. After this break, you can decide if you want to engage any further or leave the conversation for another time.

13. *Learn to Follow Up*

For many of us, when we're done with conflict, we tend not to revisit it; however, this can be problematic. By following up and checking in you ensure that everyone is satisfied with the result of the discussion. If anyone needs clarity, this would be the perfect to ask and offer clarity.

Having a process for handling conflict is always best, especially when you're starting. It offers everyone the chance to air out how they feel and can offer a solution.

Setting Boundaries

Now that we have a proper idea of how to handle conflict, we can take a look at how we can start setting boundaries. Boundaries can be defined as an invisible line that outlines what we find acceptable. Keep in mind that there are different types of boundaries which include:

Physical Boundaries

Usually when we think of physical boundaries, we're thinking about strangers; however, this is not always the case. Physical boundaries are meant to help keep us comfortable and safe even in environments that we are familiar with. For example, you may not appreciate physical affection from family and friends. So, you put in a physical boundary and label it your personal bubble. No one is meant to get into your bubble unless they have been invited.

Emotional Boundaries

Emotional boundaries are meant to help keep us comfortable and safe emotionally. They operate as a type of buffer to let people know our comfort levels when it comes to giving and receiving things emotionally. For example, you may request that sensitive issues not be discussed when you're in public spaces because it affects your emotional state.

Material and Financial Boundaries

For many of us, personal boundaries are established with our personal belongings and finances. We enforce these because we want our finances and personal belongings to be treated a certain way. For example, you may have a pair of shoes that your sibling may want to borrow. You then ask that after they use them, they put them back in the box, as you enjoy keeping your shoes in their original boxes.

Time Boundaries

Time is one of our most precious commodities because we cannot get it back. Many of us may set boundaries around our time, as we cherish it. Time boundaries could be a simple thing such as asking friends and family to show up on time or limiting the time you can spend at an outing.

Boundaries are a vital part of maintaining and building healthy relationships.

Identifying Personal Limits in Relationships

If we have smoke alarms for our homes, why don't we have alarms for when our personal boundaries are being violated? Setting and identifying personal boundaries in any relationship is vital, especially when you plan on having that relationship last for extended periods. When our personal boundaries get violated, we may feel resentment, anger, disappointment, and more. We may also feel that our trust has been broken which is a fundamental part of being in any relationship.

Before jumping into identifying your limits, it's important to remember that boundaries and limits are put in place to protect us. When coming up with limits or trying to identify your limits, you may want to start by writing down a list of the things you don't enjoy being done to you. For example, if you're not a fan of physical touch, put a boundary in place to alert those you that you are not keen on physical touch. When setting limits or identifying your limits, you'll want to remember that these are about you. This means that you have every right to state what you do and don't like.

Identifying personal limits is unique to everyone, which is why asking yourself a set of questions can help make the process a little easier. You can start by asking yourself the following questions:

- Is there anyone in your life who makes you feel scared, angry, sad, uncomfortable, or unhappy after you've spent time with them?
- What did your interaction look like with this person or people?
- Have you communicated your discomfort in the past?
- What did you think worked and what do you think didn't work?
- What do you wish was no longer said to you and how do those words or phrases make you feel?

- Has something been said to undermine your confidence and self-esteem?

The idea is to ask yourself basic questions to get a feel for what you like and don't like. Think of most of the situations that have left you uncomfortable or unable to be in certain spaces and then work from there. Although this may seem like a negative place to start, oftentimes, we are more likely to know what we don't like than what we do.

Communicating Boundaries Assertively

When communicating your boundaries, you'll want to be as assertive as possible. Being assertive simply means that you communicate your boundaries directly and honestly without having the intention of hurting another person's feelings. Communicating your boundaries does not mean that you are trying to be manipulative or controlling, it simply means that these are the boundaries for your comfort and safety.

How to Communicate Boundaries Assertively

1. Understand That These Boundaries Are About You

When communicating your boundaries, you'll want to communicate them in the first person. One of the many mistakes we make when communicating is attacking the people we communicate with through our statements. Doing things such as focusing on how they made you feel rather than simply communicating your boundaries can feel like a personal attack or an attempt to manipulate or control the situation or narrative.

2. Emphasize Consequence

Communicating our boundaries means communicating the consequences that come with violating them. When doing this always ensure that the punishment is worthy of the action. For example, perhaps you have someone who is constantly using your toothpaste, and, when it finishes, they do not replace it. Consequences for such a situation could be centered around you removing your toothpaste instead of making them move out or never speaking to them again. The action should always be worthy of the consequence no matter how emotional you may become over the issue.

3. Offer Compliments

The mood we create when communicating our boundaries is vital. What usually works is offering two compliments, one at the beginning and one at the end. This creates a type of sandwich effect with the boundary being the patty. The sandwich effect will help to regulate the situation while also minding the other person that we care about them.

Communicating our boundaries assertively is not something that has to turn ugly. In fact, we can communicate our boundaries in a respectful and caring manner. This will also make it easier for those on the receiving end of our boundaries. Keep in mind that no one wants to be told that they are hurting someone else so it's always best to tread with caution.

Respecting the Boundaries of Others

Part of having boundaries is learning to respect the boundaries of others. In this section, we cover how you can start respecting the boundaries of others.

1. *Get to Know Their Boundaries*

How do we know if we do not ask? One of the many mistakes we make is not asking about the boundaries of others. We assume that just because they aren't communicating a boundary, it doesn't exist, and this couldn't be further from the truth. By asking about boundaries, we start the conversation which could lead to us having an open discussion about our boundaries.

2. *Watch for Non-Verbal Cues*

We've already taken a deep dive into non-verbal cues and their importance. When finding out about boundaries, you'll want to take look out for non-verbal cues. These usually signal when someone is uncomfortable about a situation; however, they are unable to communicate their boundary.

3. *Empathy*

Being empathetic can be of major assistance especially when someone else is communicating a boundary. Yes, we may not have been in a similar situation; however, this doesn't stop us from understanding where they are coming from and the feelings associated with it.

4. *Be Receptive*

Communicating a boundary isn't easy, especially when you may feel as though the next person may not be receptive. By dropping our defenses and hearing where the person is coming from, you afford them the chance of feeling safe and heard.

5. *Learn About Different Experiences*

Our experiences shape our beliefs and boundaries. By understanding that everyone has a different experience from you, you can effectively afford everyone the grace to live in their truth.

6. *Acknowledge and Reflect*

Respecting someone else's boundaries is about hearing and understanding their boundary. You can do this by asking questions about their boundary to help you understand or simply reciting the boundary back to them to ensure that there are no issues.

7. *Learn to Apologize*

When we make a mistake, we take accountability for that mistake and apologize. Learning someone's boundaries isn't always easy and there may be times when you fail. When this happens ensure that you apologize and then work on remembering their boundary and doing it the right way.

During this step, you'll also want to learn to forgive yourself for violating their boundary. Oftentimes, the pain of violating a boundary is what causes us to withdraw. By forgiving yourself and learning to do better, you afford yourself grace.

8. *Ask for Help*

When we're continuously violating a boundary, it's best to seek professional help to assist us in seeing what the problem may be. There is no shame in asking for assistance especially when it involves those we love and care about.

Setting boundaries and respecting boundaries can be tricky; however, it is necessary. Understand that this is a learning process and that you won't get it right every single time. This will help alleviate the pressure that comes with doing something new.

The Role of Boundaries in Maintaining Healthy Relationships

Throughout this chapter, we have mentioned and spoken about boundaries, how to set them, and how to respect the boundaries of others. During this time, we've also seen that boundaries can play a positive role in reinforcing who we are and what we stand for. So, what role do boundaries have in maintaining a healthy relationship?

Setting boundaries in any social relationship is vital, especially when you do not want the relationship to become toxic, unsatisfactory, or for your overall well-being to suffer. This is because when our boundaries are not respected, we may feel as though we are not seen, loved, or cared for causing us to become resentful.

By setting healthy boundaries, you can:

- reduce codependency while increasing autonomy
- set your expectations
- encourage emotional, physical, mental, financial, and spiritual safety among yourself and others
- feel empowered and worthy of respect
- set and enforce individual responsibility
- and be able to separate your thoughts, wants, and needs from the feelings of others

When we create healthy boundaries and respect the boundaries of others, we're able to function as needed within our social health. We're also able to build and maintain our relationships without feeling as though we are burdened by anyone and their thoughts, options, and feelings. This means that boundaries play a vital part in keeping our relationships healthy and functioning.

Now that we understand the basics and foundations of building healthy social relationships, we need to move on to how we can start developing meaningful connections. Come with us as we take a look at how you can develop meaningful connections by initiating new relationships, deepening existing relationships, and diversifying your social circle.

DEVELOPING MEANINGFUL CONNECTIONS

Initiating New Relationships

The first step to having good social relationships is building them. This means that you'll need to initiate new relationships. In this section, we focus on the different strategies you can use to approach new people, how to build trust, and how to overcome rejection.

Strategies for Approaching New People

Making friends and starting friendships can prove to be challenging. Below we offer you a strategy to assist you in your pursuit of making new friends and building healthy relationships.

1. *Start With a Friendly Greeting*

First impressions are everything, especially when trying to form social relationships. The best way to create a good first impression is to start with a friendly greeting.

People are drawn to kind and warm people. When your greeting is warm and kind, it offers you the chance to present yourself as friendly and approachable. This means that even when another encounter takes place, you are the first familiar and friendly face they run to thus forming a relationship.

Keep in mind that a large population of people suffer from anxiety, so being friendly and warm can assist them in lowering their defenses and enable them to engage more easily with you.

2. *Introduce Yourself*

Although this may seem obvious, it is not something people tend to do first. Instead, we may strike up conversation or find it awkward to introduce ourselves. The longer we wait to introduce ourselves, the more anxiety builds up, causing us to withdraw, which can negatively affect our ability to engage in conversation. By introducing yourself, you get the formalities out of the way. Be sure to repeat the person's name before you end the conversation. This can help you remember it and may add sentimental value to the conversation.

3. *Ask Questions*

One of the best ways to strike up a conversation is by asking a question. When asking a question, it's always best to ask an open-ended question, as this allows for the other party to explain themselves or offer context. It also affords them the chance to ask you questions and hear about your thoughts and feelings toward a certain topic.

Asking questions is an amazing way to engage in conversation and start friendships. It also assists you with finding out what you may have in common. Don't be afraid to ask questions and engage in conversation especially when trying to build healthy and functioning social relationships.

4. *Don't be Afraid to Comment on Something*

Striking up a conversation can prove difficult when you're meeting someone or people for the first time. Usually, after a while, things tend to go silent. It's at this point that the conversation may turn awkward, and everyone may not know what to do.

When this happens, don't be afraid to talk about something that stands out to you. It could be anything! As long as you have something positive to say and you find it interesting, it can work as a conversation piece.

5. *Pretend That You're Already Friends*

Oftentimes, our mindset is what is keeping us from making friends and having conversations. Something that works well is pretending that you're already friends with the person you're trying to speak to. This can help lessen pressure and overall anxiety, which can lead to a calm mind. Think of your already existing relationships, what do you say to your friends?

The key is to be as natural as possible. Forming relationships on something that you are not can and will backfire. It's always best to be as genuine as possible.

6. Use Shared Struggles

One of the best ways to strike up conversation is by bringing up a shared struggle. Perhaps you work under the same horrible manager or are constantly late for work. Either way, using struggle or a shared experience is always a good way to strike up conversation. It shows that you guys can relate to each other on some level and can lead to further discussions.

7. Use Personal Observation

Compliments are an amazing conversation starter. It shows someone that there's something you like about them. By offering a compliment or a kind word, we automatically get pushed into the nice category.

8. Use Positive Non-verbal Cues

In the previous chapter, we learned the importance of non-verbal cues and how important it is for your body language to be in agreement with your speech. With this being said, you'll want to maintain positive body language throughout your conversation including maintaining eye contact, keeping a safe distance, and having an open posture. These ensure that you are non-threatening and can make others feel comfortable around you.

9. Enthusiasm

Showing enthusiasm is a great way to connect with others. It shows them that we're willing to engage and that we're excited to meet them. When showing enthusiasm, you'll want to ensure that your body language is also in agreement. Doing things such as showing hand signals, raising your hand, or simply pointing at something can be an effective way to gain attention.

You'll also want to remain alert for things like hand gestures and signals from others. In these situations, it can also be appropriate to use body language or signs to respond.

10. *Afford Everyone the Chance to Speak*

Being the life of the party is amazing; however, affording everyone to have their chance to speak is vital especially when you're trying to make new friends. Engage in the conversation and don't talk too much or too little. Remember, this conversation is meant to flow and feel as natural as possible.

One of the many things you can do at this time is to play conversation Jenga. Allow for everyone to build on the points of what the other has said. By doing this, everyone is afforded space to exist in the conversation and can feel as though they contributed toward it.

11. *Be Helpful*

A great way to strike up conversation and build social relationships is to be helpful. When we're helpful, we're able to spot the needs of others and approach them in a nice way. This could lead to each one of you doing favors for the next, which can lead to amazing social relationships.

12. *Be Curious*

Yes, curiosity may have killed the cat; however, when trying to build social relationships, curiosity is an amazing conversation starter. So many of us, when trying to start a conversation, get stuck in our heads. We end up trying to find the right moment to speak, resulting in us not saying at all. Allowing ourselves to be curious means allowing ourselves to speak and engage in conversation.

Starting conversations and engaging with others can turn into a nightmare, especially when you're trying to push yourself outside of your comfort zone. The idea is to attempt and to continue to attempt until you find and perfect your way of doing things.

Building Rapport and Trust From the Beginning

Now that we know how to engage and start a conversation, we need to focus on how we can start building our rapport and trust. To do this effectively, we need to understand the meaning of rapport and trust.

Trust can be described as a type of assurance when it comes to ability, character, strength, and even truth toward someone or something. Some psychologists may deem trust as a set of behaviors or beliefs in the probability of someone behaving or acting in a certain way. We can trust in ourselves, a religious leader, friends, bosses, accountants, and more. For many, trust is built over time, with some struggling to trust others due to past issues.

Rapport refers to the closeness and harmony of a relationship. Usually, the people involved in this type of relationship have mutual understanding, respect, and are mostly in agreement. When seeking to build rapport, it's always best to understand that these take time and dedication meaning that it may take longer than expected; however, there are a few things that you can do to help you along the way.

Building relationships is not something that comes easy, which is why many of us may struggle to build rapport and trust. Below we offer you a few tips to help you along the way.

Tactics to Build Rapport and Trust

Be Aware of the Impact of First Impressions

Although we can change people's impressions of us, first impressions may be long-lasting and can be a determining factor as to whether or not people want to engage with us.

One such example is the halo effect. The halo effect is described as a cognitive bias that showcases the link between positive impressions of brands, people, or even businesses and our overall feelings towards a particular person, place, business, and more. Simply placed, how we show up is vital and can influence how people may feel about us in other areas.

When dealing with people, you'll want to think of the halo effect and understand that how you show up can have a serious impact on what people think of you.

Exercise Active Listening

Think of the last time you engaged in conversation with someone who constantly interrupted you. Did you feel seen, valued, or heard? Was there any frustration experienced in that conversation and would you engage in another conversation with that person?

Conversation is about offering the next person a chance to contribute. Part of building trust is showing that you're willing to listen and afford those you engage with the chance to share their values and opinions. To do this you'll need to implement good listening skills.

Ask Questions That Allow Engagement

Much like our previous point, having a conversation is about engagement and sharing experiences between people. Many times, we're afraid to approach conversation because we fear rejection.

A good way to start a conversation is by asking open-ended questions. This will afford the person you're trying to engage with the opportunity to speak and even ask questions.

When trying to ask open-ended questions, you'll want to start by asking yourself why you want to engage in conversation with them. What about them has made you want to converse? What would you like to know about them and why?

This will lay out a type of blueprint to assist you in creating conversation and keeping both parties engaged.

Be Aware of Non-verbal Cues

Non-verbal cues contribute 55% of how our conversation is received (Mind Tools Content Team). When trying to engage in conversation, you'll want to think of how you conduct yourself. Using excessive non-verbal cues can come across as overly excited and can chase prospects away. Do your best to remain as engaging as possible.

Find Common Ground

Engaging in conversation with someone new is easily one of the most awkward experiences we may have. We may find ourselves caving in after asking two questions and wondering if we have something in common.

The first few sentences are never the right place to give up on conversation. The more we speak to people, the more we find that we share common experiences or feelings. The idea is to keep talking until we find common ground and work our way up from there.

Have Empathy and Respect

To build rapport and trust we first need to start by working on empathy and respect. In a way, we need to treat others how we would want to be treated, which is respectfully. Having a conversation is about engaging in the depths of emotions that can lead to sincere sharing and ultimately a sincere relationship. By offering empathy and respect, you afford someone the chance to be understood and the opportunity to share their experience.

One of the many things that can keep us from building sincere relationships is the fear of rejection. In the next section, we cover how you can overcome the fear of rejection.

Overcoming the Fear of Rejection

Intimating conversation or anything having to do with something new can be daunting and can bring up feelings of anxiety, discomfort, and panic. By overcoming your fears, you get over anxiety, discomfort, and panic making it easier to form connections.

Usually, the fear of rejection stems from our innate longing for social acceptance and belonging. We may find that our fear of rejection is heightened during pivotal moments such as rejection from potential or current spouses, during job applications, or simply while reaching out to obtain any of our desires. This accompanied by past traumatic experiences that can be found in our adulthood, childhood, or even during our teenage years can cause a long-lasting impact that makes us sensitive to all, if not many, forms of rejection. In addition to this, we may also find ourselves living in fear and constant panic due to societal norms and pressures on what certain aspects of our lives should look like. These can have a profound impact on our self-esteem and may cause us to speak poorly of ourselves and our capabilities thus reinforcing the fear of rejection and unhealthy societal norms.

For many of us, we may struggle to handle rejection, which can be attributed to many reasons. One of the reasons is that our self-esteem is closely tied to the approval and appreciation of others. This means that when people do not approve of our actions or reject our ideas, it tends to take a toll on our self-worth. In addition to this, we may be seeking perfection, meaning that we view rejection as failure instead of seeing it as a normal part of life or a learning curve. Other reasons could include that we have not had the chance to build our resistance toward rejection, meaning that we are unable to handle it or find a healthy coping mechanism.

Keep in mind that your fear of rejection could also be heightened by depression or anxiety. Usually, when we're in these states it makes us hyper-sensitive in all aspects of our lives and could push us further into the abyss of loneliness and overall inability to form and maintain new friendships and relationships.

The fear of rejection can manifest in many ways. Here are eight signs that you may struggle with the fear of rejection:

- You tend to avoid social situations, which include gatherings, job interviews, or anything that would be done in a group setting.
- There is a constant fear of expressing your feelings toward a certain situation because you fear that you will be rejected.
- You constantly seek approval or reassurance from others.

- Perfectionism is something you strive toward so that you can avoid making mistakes or feeling as though you fall short.
- You engage in self-talk, which contributes toward a negative self-image.
- There is a tendency to people please, especially when you're trying to avoid rejection and gain acceptance.
- You may struggle with issues concerning criticism, whether friendly or not, because it brings up feelings of inadequacy.
- Fear of rejection can manifest in an inability to express your thoughts, ideas, values, and emotions openly.

So, how do we overcome our fear of rejection?

How to Overcome the Fear of Rejection

Now that we understand what fear can do, it's time to look into how we can overcome the fear of rejection.

Acknowledge How You Feel

For many of us, the pain of rejection is too much to bear, especially when it's connected to a traumatic experience. Unfortunately, rejection is something that we must live through and conquer. By acknowledging your feelings, you give yourself room to accept the rejection while understanding that it has nothing to do with your self-worth. How many times you get looked over has nothing to do with how valuable and worthy you are as a person. When we detach our value from the opportunities we get and the amount of rejection we receive, we're able to see our self-worth a lot more clearly.

Challenge Your Inner Thoughts

Who is the person behind your inner thoughts? Would you repeat your negative self-talk to someone else? Oftentimes, our greatest fears are simply a manifestation of a traumatic experience that left our inner voice paralyzed. By challenging our inner thoughts, we're able to challenge the reality of our thoughts. When we do this, we often ask questions centered around how real our thoughts are. If the thought is not a fact, then it may not be a reality or the outcome of the situation.

Practice Compassion

Nothing great or sustainable can be achieved in an environment that is polluted with self-hate. Not being compassionate toward one's self is a recipe for disaster as it destroys our self-image and ability to stay motivated and inspired. By practicing compassion toward ourselves we are afforded the chance to see our greatness.

Build Resilience

When we build our resilience, we're able to build a type of defense against rejection. Instead of diminishing our self-worth, we're able to understand that this was simply not our opportunity and that another one will come.

Face Your Fear

Bravery is not the absence of fear but rather our ability to see a need or want and push through despite our fear. When seeking success in life, you'll want to know and understand that fear will come into play. The more we expose ourselves to fear, the less we will feel as though it is uncharted ground. Facing your fears is an amazing way to deal with rejection, especially when it's something you struggle with constantly. When reaching the other side of fear, you'll want to heed the outcome. The more you know that things aren't as bad as they seem, the more you'll try to take more chances.

Use It as an Opportunity to Learn and Grow

Rejection provides the perfect opportunity for us to grow. When we're rejected, we get to learn more about ourselves and the situation while possibly finding ways to do better in the future. Keep in mind that when you fail and try again, you're failing with experience, meaning that you won't be starting over because now you'll have experience.

Ask for Support

For many of us, when rejection comes knocking, we don't let others know that we need support. This is one of the biggest mistakes you can make, as those we love can remind us that we're worth something. Ask for support and don't be ashamed to ask for it because it can help keep you going.

Take Care of Yourself

Self-care is vital when pushing through an experience involving fear. You can do simple things such as engage in something you enjoy like reading a book, booking a massage or even taking a walk. The point is to take care of yourself while you take care of the fear. This is because this transition can greatly affect your mental health.

Seek Professional Help

Since rejection may be strongly rooted in a traumatic experience, you'll want to ensure that you seek professional help. Dealing with fear is also about dealing with the root of the fear.

Seeing a professional has nothing to do with your ability to handle the situation but everything to do with equipping yourself. If you'd never go to war with just your fists, then you should never face mental or emotional issues without the necessary guidance.

Deepening Existing Relationships

Sometimes, the relationships we seek are already among us all we need to do is invest in them. In this section, we focus on how you can deepen your already existing relationships.

Investing Time and Effort: The Key to Deeper Connections

Creating and building connections will require that we maintain that connection. For many of us, we find ourselves already amid good social connections; however, we're struggling to deepen those connections. By investing effort into those relationships, we find ourselves creating space for those we care about. In this section, we focus on how you can invest time and effort into your already existing connections causing them to become deeper.

Start With the Basics

Think of your social relationships as a garden. The less time we spend in the garden, the more we'll need to work on it when we return. We may find things like weeds, some of our plants may have died and we'll find that we tire ourselves out trying to fix the damage. The same can be said for social relationships and their maintenance. The more time we spend away from the people we engage with, the wider the gap between us grows. We may find that we overwork ourselves trying to close the gap.

Going back to basics simply means that we work on reconnecting and rebuilding. This entails us getting to know each other again, meaning that we touch base with whatever is happening in our lives. Depending on the type of relationship you have, you may discuss the reason behind the separation and the different ways you can work on bridging the gap.

Look Into Your Foundation of Connection

Without connection, our relationships would hold no depth and emotional attachment. Connection in the relationship simply means that there is mutual understanding, emotional intimacy, and shared experiences. By dedicating time to look into our connection, we show the other party that this relationship is important and that we are willing to strengthen, commit, care, and prioritize this relationship.

Rebuild Trust and Security

One of the simplest ways to rebuild trust and security within a relationship is to offer time. This creates a sense of reliability and dependability within the relationship. By consistently showing up for the next person, remaining consistent, offering support, listening, and showing care we build trust within the relationship and our willingness to make it work.

Strengthen Communication and Understanding

Communication and understanding is one of the most important things needed in a relationship. When we maintain communication, we can rebuild and deepen a once-dormant relationship. Communication has to be open and honest to achieve the desired result, which is a deeper understanding of each other's thoughts, feelings, and needs. By having meaningful conversations, we can gauge needs and act accordingly.

Create Shared Memories and Experiences

Relationships are about creating memories and experiences. When we invest time to create shared experiences and memories, we tighten the already existing bond between ourselves.

To do this, you'll want to think of something that both of you are interested in or have been meaning to do. The aim is to enjoy yourselves while also being in the present moment.

When we think of relationships, we need to think of the resources at our disposal. Things such as time and effort are resources that can be used to help reinforce our connection and create something deeper.

Understanding and Respecting Differences

Entering into social relationships means being exposed to different cultures, childhood experiences, opinions, and more. For many, this can cause conflict, resulting in issues within the relationship and other parties feeling as though their personal experiences, values, and beliefs are disregarded. To avoid this issue, you'll want to understand and respect the differences you may see in others. So, how do we understand and respect the differences of others?

1. Start by acknowledging your differences. Many times, when we're faced with a difference in opinion, we tend to dismiss it. The idea is that difference equates to disagreements, which is not always the case. Having a difference in upbringing, opinions, childhood and other aspects of life is a teachable moment because we get to see

what the world looks like in the eyes of another. By accepting differences and using them as opportunities to learn we can set the tone for understanding and respect which can help to ensure that those we engage with feel seen, valued, and respected.

2. Laying the foundation for respect and understanding starts with empathy. When we're empathetic, we're able to come from a point of understanding rather than looking at the difference as an obstacle or stumbling block. Remember that everyone deserves to be heard and understood, especially when it comes to their experience.

3. Our ability to communicate our can either hinder or enhance our ability to understand and respect the differences of others. In Chapter 2, we focused on the art of communication and the different things we can do to ensure that we communicate effectively. Remember, sometimes it isn't about what you say but rather how you say it that can distort a message. While communicating, you'll want to discuss any boundaries you may feel are necessary. When doing so, you'll want to ensure that you are not focused on attacking but that your tone is assertive.

4. To understand and respect something we must educate ourselves on that particular subject. This means that to understand the differences of our friends, family, colleagues, or others, we must educate ourselves on the matter at hand. Even when more information has been acquired, it's important to understand that we do not have all the answers. There may be a few gaps in our information, meaning that we should address the situation with an open mind and willingness to learn something new. Keep in mind that our perspective and mindset play a major role in our ability to understand and respect something. When we view something as not making sense, are overly critical, or dismissive, we tend to disrespect and undermine the beliefs and values of others. By changing our mindset, we also alter our attitude.

Our relationships benefit from mutual respect and understanding. This is because we afford the people in our circle a safe space to express their views and opinions. When we offer respect and understanding, we set the tone of the entire relationship which can be centered around respect and understanding.

The Importance of Shared Experiences and Memories

For many of us, when we think of social relationships, we're usually thinking about shared experiences and memories. Shared experiences and memories help to create a personal attachment to relationships while simultaneously assisting the relationship to grow. So what are shared memories and experiences and do we have to be there physically to create them?

A shared experience can be described as a moment where all parties are present, engaged, and participating. Those involved in the moment do not have to physically be together to experience it; however, they need to be present mentally and emotionally. The idea is to experience the moment with you and be fully aware of what's happening and why.

The Benefits of Shared Experiences and Memories

It is never the experience but rather the people we create memories with who leave an impact. Having positive experiences can increase our feelings of connection, belonging, and meaning, which can help with self-esteem and also decrease feelings of depression, anxiety, and isolation.

For many of us, when we think of such experiences, we're usually thinking of creating them with people we know. Thankfully, we can achieve the same results even when creating memories with strangers. Creating memories with strangers can operate as a learning curve, offering us new experiences that can help us learn from others.

Overall, shared experiences can contribute to our mental and emotional health while also helping us foster empathy. Keep in mind that sharing these experiences can also contribute positively toward our overall health and life satisfaction.

Maximizing the Power of Shared Experiences and Memories

We can only experience the benefit of something when we use and maximize its power. The same can be said for shared memories and experiences; we need to maximize our shared experiences and memories.

Maximizing your shared experiences and memories means using every opportunity to interact with others as best as you can. In a world where technology has replaced human interaction, every opportunity to engage with others should be used as best as possible. So, how do we maximize our shared experiences and memories?

Learn to Leverage Your Time

One of the many stumbling blocks we may experience when trying to connect with others is issues with time. The cost of living has become so high that many have taken to using their free time to generate an income for themselves. This means working two or three jobs at a time, meaning that there is less time for social activities and socializing as a whole.

When we learn to leverage our time, we learn to socialize even amid busyness. We can achieve this through multitasking, which can help you incorporate socialization into your hectic work schedule. For example, taking a lunch break offers us the opportunity to refuel and refocus; however, it's also an opportunity for social engagement. Sharing a meal has always been an amazing way to engage while also assisting to create conversation and shared memories and experiences. The beautiful thing about this experience is that the two of you don't have to be in the same space to do this. You can simply schedule a video call and share the experience.

Learn to Shake Things Up

Getting into a social routine is amazing; however, we may find ourselves in sticky situations, such as a co-worker we usually have lunch with is going on vacation. During these times, you'll want to try and schedule a lunch call with another co-worker. Doing something simple such as inviting them for a coffee, even if it's virtual, can assist in getting the ball rolling. The idea is to keep things interesting and allow yourself to experience something new.

Shaking things up could also mean taking a work trip with your colleagues. Usually, in these circumstances, we may find that we are inclined to choose team-building exercises that can not only strengthen the team but also assist with fostering a bond. By changing the environment, you could also be changing their mindsets, which can assist in making others feel comfortable and encourage social interaction.

Remember, every interaction will be different and while trying to get it right you may get it wrong. Use the trial-and-error method to gauge whether what you're doing is working and whether or not it's sustainable. The idea is to do things that you can sustain and that do not make you or anyone else feel uncomfortable.

Balancing Independence With Interdependence

Deepening our current social relationships means finding a balance between independence and interdependence. To find the balance, we must first understand what independence and interdependence mean.

Independence can be described and defined as a state of wanting and or having the capability to do something yourself. For example, you may be faced with an important decision to make. Exercising independence means that you can decide without influence or pressure from those around you or those involved in the situation. This means that the decision made is solely based on your personal needs and wants.

Interdependence, on the other hand, can be described and defined as a mutual reliance on someone else. In layman's terms, both parties rely on each other to achieve or maintain a certain goal. This goal could be anything including maintaining the relationship.

Finding the Balance

Building and maintaining healthy and functional relationships is all about balance. In this case, finding a balance between independence and interdependence. To keep our relationships healthy, we need to focus on ourselves while also maintaining a deep connection within our social relationships. In this section, we focus on finding the balance between the two to help you live a more balanced life.

Uniqueness in Self

For many of us, when we enter into relationships or find a connection, we lose ourselves trying to maintain it. When entering into a new connection or relationship of any kind, we need to maintain our personal boundaries, objectives, interests, goals, and growth even if they come into conflict with those we are in a relationship with. The goal is to ensure that we maintain our own identity which can help to promote self-assurance and autonomy.

Think of a situation where you have abandoned yourself to maintain the relationship. You lost your identity, goals, interests, hobbies, and other things that were associated with who you were to pick up the new identity that can only be found in that connection. Now think of what happens when there's separation. This automatically means that the identity you've picked up to serve that person is no longer your own as you cannot maintain it without them. The vision of who you are and what you stand for has been lost because they have left.

Maintaining your own identity is about more than just remaining the same. It's a direct link between you, your personal growth, and the people and relationships you maintain. When we're able to hold onto our identity, we're able to exist in the relationship as an individual and as a couple, friend, sister, co-worker, and more.

Respecting Individuality

Being in a relationship with someone is also about respecting their individuality. To do this, we need to respect that they have interests, goals, and objectives of their own that, in many cases, are not a threat to the relationship.

When we find ways to celebrate our partner's uniqueness, we find a way to not only understand them but support them in their endeavors. True love is about affording your partner the chance to blossom and see how far their talents, skills, knowledge, and gifts can take them. It's about offering them the freedom they need to live their life.

Developing a Shared Identity in the Relationship

Although independence is important in a relationship, it's always important to remember that relationships are held together by interdependence. This is because all parties involved are reliant on the other to make the relationship work. Interdependence is vital especially when it comes to the delegation of tasks and authority, accepting responsibility, and reaching a general agreement on issues happening within the relationship.

It's always important to check on whether or not the interdependence in your relationship is healthy. Unhealthy interdependence can lead to codependency, which means that one or all parties sacrifice themselves and their identity to make the relationship work. In other instances, you may be enabling unhealthy behavior or habits. Either way, codependency can lead to severe consequences that can negatively impact the lives of those involved or destroy the relationship. To avoid such issues, it's always important to foster a relationship that celebrates individuality but also offers a joint identity. Striking a balance between the two is vital as an imbalance can lead to the relationship falling apart.

Societal Norms and Relationships

In a previous section, we took a look at how our environment can influence our ability to reason and the lens we use to see the world. The same can be said for societal norms, which influence how we conduct ourselves and the opinions and views we have of the world and environment around us. This means that societal norms affect how we function in relationships and can have a direct or indirect influence on the way we view interdependence and independence within the context of relationships or social relationships as a whole.

Keep in mind that societal norms may differ from country to country, religion to religion, culture to culture, and so forth. Some cultures may support personal growth and self-reliance, while others may promote interdependence, which can and mostly does have ties to the community and family members.

Although societal norms operate as a type of framework for relationships and social engagements, we need to constantly evaluate whether or not they benefit our current relationships and the impact they are having. The idea is to think of our boundaries and find out whether the current societal norms fit in with our boundaries. Usually, these types of discussions are had with all those involved in the relationship to assist in ensuring that all parties are aware of personal boundaries concerning societal norms. Doing this can encourage us to find a balance within our relationship that promotes personal development, which results in the relationship being rewarding and respectful. In the end, our aim is for both parties is to feel loved, respected, valued, seen, and heard.

Diverse Social Circles

A social circle can be defined as a group of people who interact with each other and may share similar characteristics or interests while also having a sense of unity. In this section, we take a deeper look into social circles, their importance, and how you can overcome prejudices that come with being a diverse social circle.

The Benefits of Having a Diverse Group of Friends

The word diversity can be described as something that has or is composed of different elements. Diversity within the context of relationships is described as the quality or practice of including individuals from different spectrums, which include socio-economic backgrounds, religions, cultures, races, and more. When our friend group is diverse, we have the opportunity to challenge what we know to be true about the world. It poses an opportunity for us to learn, grow, and develop while seeing the world through the eyes of another. So, what are the benefits of having a diverse friend group?

Wider Spectrum

For many of us, we tend to experience the world through the lenses we were given by our experiences. This means that our experiences create our reality, hence we have certain opinions, beliefs, values, and goals.

When we have a diverse friend group, we automatically open ourselves up to new experiences and opinions. Of course, we do not have to change who we are; however, it can give us insight into the world and experiences of others. This can help us think creatively while also offering us more meaningful connections.

Interaction Improvement

The more diverse friendships we have, the easier we may find it to interact with others. This is because we have been exposed to other cultures, beliefs, societal norms, and ways of thinking. When this happens, we tend to put aside any biases we may have had and become more open to future or present interactions with others.

Improved Mental Health

One of the many things we may experience within a diverse friendship group is validation. When we go through struggle and pain, it is hard for us to find those who can sympathize with our grief or loss. By interacting with a diverse group of people, we may find those who can understand our situation and experience, thus making us feel seen, heard, and valued. This can help to deepen our relationships and improve our self-image while also improving our mental health.

Better Advice

Coming from different situations means having different ideologies and philosophies on different topics. When we have a diverse friendship group, we're able to seek advice and support from different individuals with different ideas. This can help us come up with a proper solution to many of the problems we may face.

There are various benefits that come with having a diverse friend group. The idea is to harness the power of diversity by learning from those around you.

Overcoming Prejudices and Embracing Diversity

To overcome prejudice, we first need to understand what it is. Prejudice can be described as a favor or dislike of something or someone without any just cause. It can show up as an intense feeling toward a group of people based on preconceived ideas of how they behave or who they associate with. Keep in mind that prejudice can either be negative or positive depending on the situation at hand. The idea is that we favor or dislike someone causing us to not see the situation. This can lead to poor judgment or can hinder our ability to engage with a diverse group of people. So, how do we overcome prejudice?

Start by Being Self-Aware

Being aware of who we are and the experiences that have helped to shape us plays a major role in how we perceive others. This is because we have an understanding of how our experiences influence our thinking, behavior, mannerisms, and more. When we think this way, we're able to understand how people may be a product of their environment and not necessarily their current circumstances. This affords us the chance to see them as they are as opposed to seeing them through the lens of prejudice, allowing us to embrace diversity.

Focus on What You Have in Common

Instead of focusing on the differences you may share, start by focusing on what you may have in common. By focusing on commonality and shared experiences, you can shift your focus from what is different to what may be the same. This can spark conversation and make all parties feel comfortable. From this point, we can share our differences in experience, upbringing, and so forth.

Be Respectful

For many of us, we hold our experiences, opinions, values, beliefs, and goals very dear to our hearts. This means that a difference in opinion centered around such topics can result in an argument and hurt feelings. To engage with a diverse group of people we must understand that this construct, even though it is true for ourselves, is also true for others. Approaching differences in a respectful, calm, and understanding manner can help us to see past prejudice as it affords the next person the chance to explain their reality. Remember; the truth may be subjective to how we view the world. This means that although we may have preconceived ideas they are not facts but opinions especially when it comes to the experiences of others.

Get Involved

Interaction is one of the best ways to overcome prejudice. When we're actively involved with others while doing something we love, we can develop the ability to see people as individuals and not necessarily what we associate them with. In some cases, getting involved could be traveling to a different country to experience the culture or simply visiting someone in their home. The idea is to place yourself in their spaces and expose yourself to what they have been exposed to to grasp how they became who they are. This is to help you gain some form of context, which can allow you to overcome prejudice.

Overcoming prejudice takes work, especially when your main aim is to try and understand. By being respectful, getting involved, and focusing on what you have in common, you can start your journey toward diversity.

Learning From Different Perspectives and Experiences

To interact effectively with a diverse group of people, we'll need to learn from different perspectives and experiences. Various benefits come with learning from different perspectives which include:

- gaining a better understanding
- seeing a problem from different angles
- letting go of judgment, stereotypical thinking, and prejudice and focusing on facts
- keeping and maintaining a balanced viewpoint
- thinking and acting rationally
- being objective and unbiased
- reduces stress
- develops empathy
- works as a learning experience
- contributed to personal growth
- and helps to gain clarity

To fully experience the benefits of learning from different perspectives and experiences, we need to teach ourselves how we can learn from them.

How to Learn From Different Perspectives and Experiences

In a previous section, we took a look at how our experiences have a direct link to the way we view the world. Although this is true, it is not the only thing that influences our perspective. Perspective is influenced by experience, whether past, present, or at first glance. This means that we can change our perspective, thus changing how we may be experiencing the world. A great way to start changing our perspective is by embracing diversity.

Diversity plays a major role in how we view the world. When we embrace diversity, we widen our scope and change the narrative of our thinking. This is because embracing diversity challenges our current thinking process through new information.

Embracing diversity does not mean that we are silent and accepting but rather we are gathering information and asking questions to understand. When we ask questions, we hear different perspectives and experiences, thus we are learning from different perspectives and experiences.

When wanting to learn from the experiences of others, you'll want to make a habit of being open-minded. This does not mean that you lose yourself trying to learn but rather that you step into everything with the willingness to learn something new.

During this process, you'll want to think about all your blind spots. Blind spots can hinder our ability to see things as they are. The more you embrace diversity, the more blind spots you may find. By working on your blind spots, you can make the learning process a lot easier.

Focusing on the facts at hand instead of focusing on what you already know can help you not become overly emotional. This can ensure that you are level-headed while also making sure that you're personal feelings are not in the way of your learning.

Embracing diversity and learning from the experiences and perspectives of others can become challenging when we don't know where to draw the line. This could mean becoming overly emotional over certain information or forcing others to believe that their experiences and perspectives are wrong. To avoid this, learn to draw a line between fact and opinion while also knowing when you need to stop fighting.

Learning is a process, with many of us learning new information every day. With the aid of technology, we're able to see the world through the eyes of others while having the ability to contact them and ask them about their experiences and perspectives. In the next chapter, we will take a deeper look into the digital dimension.

THE DIGITAL DIMENSION

Social Media and Relationships

Technology has changed the way we interact through the introduction of social media platforms. In this section, we take a deeper look into social media and the effect it is having on relationships.

Navigating the Pros and Cons of Social Media in Relationships

Social media platforms were created with the intent of making communication and keeping in touch easier. The idea was to create an online platform that allowed for images, videos, and communication to be shared across a network of people. Since then, social media has evolved to become a place of entertainment, business, networking, support groups, and more.

In recent times, we've also seen the idea of relationships change with today's relationships being called modern relationships. To understand the impact that social media has had on relationships, we'll need to understand what the modern relationship is.

Have you ever taken the time to analyze how relationships, along with their values, have changed over the last 50 years? If so, what stood out to you the most about the changes? Did you think of power dynamics and the role each gender played in their relationship? What are your thoughts on traditional relationships, and do you believe that men and women were happy and satisfied in these roles?

We ask because the narrative surrounding relationships, including their values, gender roles, and more, has changed drastically. In marriages, both parties are responsible for bringing money into the relationship. This means that both parties are held equally accountable and liable for the role they play in the relationship. Modern relationships are comprised of mutual understanding and respect.

Most modern relationships will have different dynamics. The more we understand modern relationships and their dynamics, the easier we can understand the role that social media plays. Modern relationships can come in the form of

- cohabiting partners
- open relationships
- long-distance relationships
- virtual relationships, and more

Although the dynamics of relationships have changed, their foundations have not. These include trust, commitment, and honesty. These three core pillars are vital in any relationship, whether it be friendship, family bond, or any other social tie. The influence of social media on relationships can be found with pros and cons.

Pros of Social Media in Relationships

There are various pros that come with using social media.

Networking

Social media offers us a chance to network and possibly find a long-lasting friendship or relationship. We can simply go on social media platforms and proceed to directly message those we believe would be a perfect fit. Additionally, we may be able to video call them and set up virtual dates which can help us along the way.

Networking can also take place through dating apps, which are specifically designed to assist us find that special one. All things considered, social media plays a major role in our ability to find people who have similar interests.

Communication

Social media is well known for its ability to offer us easy communication. We can keep in contact with family members, friends, co-workers, and spouses using social media platforms. This is because they allow for video calls, the sending of messages, the sharing of images, and so much more. Communication is a stable internet connection away, making it easier to keep in touch with our family members.

Record, Tag, and Share Experiences

Social media affords us the chance to record, tag, and share our experiences with those in our network. Partners, friends, co-workers, and even acquaintances can share images and videos, instantly making memories and experiences that much more memorable.

Online Support and Advice

For many of us, social media is the perfect place for us to get advice and support. We can submit our stories anonymously and have strangers weigh in on our issues. We can also find support groups that can offer the support we need through shared experiences.

Understanding

Have you ever wanted to find out more about someone and then rushed to their social media platform? Social media affords us the chance to get to know our partners, their beliefs, values, sense of humor, and more through posts and shared posts.

We instantly become more aware of who someone is due to what they post. We can also gauge whether or not they will be a perfect fit for who we are and the things we stand for.

We can also join similar groups that can explain their interests in-depth for us to have better knowledge. The possibilities with social media are endless.

Negative Impact of Social Media on Relationships

In as much as there are positive aspects of social media, there are also negative aspects.

Increase in Jealousy and Insecurity

Social media can play a major role in facilitating jealousy and insecurity within your relationships. We may become jealous of friends, family, or even co-workers due to their lifestyle and following.

In relationships, we may feel as though we are inadequate because of the attention our partner may be receiving on social media. Social media provides opportunities for mistrust, communication issues, and many more problems.

Ideally, we're meant to speak to our partners about social media and the boundaries we have in place.

Comparison

One of the many things we may find is that we compare ourselves to others. Due to social media being so open, we're able to see what is happening in the lives of others. This can cause us to compare ourselves and also instigate self-hatred, anxiety, depression, low self-esteem, and more.

Due to comparison, we may find ourselves forcing our partners to do things they are not used to doing. This can lead to issues in the relationship, which can ultimately cause a breakup.

Unrealistic Expectations

This ties in with our previous point on comparison. A lot of the time, what we're exposed to on social media has been curated. There have been hours spent on filming and getting just the right shot to sell a dream, story, or product. Some have even gone to the lengths of renting apartments, cars, and other items to create a reality that you are exposed to.

Unfortunately, this creates unrealistic expectations of what life should look like. When this happens, not only are we comparing ourselves, but we're also putting those we love under pressure to match a standard that truly does not exist.

Infidelity

Social media platforms, although they offer us access to vital information, expose us to infidelity. In today's age, cheating has become a norm, with many being forced to look through social media platforms to find the truth about what their partner is doing.

Addiction

For many of us, social media has become our addiction, with many of us getting easily distracted by notifications from our favorite social media apps. The problem is we're spending more time with social media than our actual partners. This can lead our partners to experience feelings of loneliness while also believing that you simply do not care.

Social media plays both good and bad cop. Depending on how we use it and the boundaries we set up, we can either make or break our relationships.

Understanding the Impact of Digital Footprints

To understand the impact of a digital footprint, we first need to understand what a digital footprint is. A digital footprint, also known as a digital shadow or electronic footprint, is the trail of data we leave behind when we access the internet. It includes all digital activities such as sending emails, visiting websites, submitting online information, and more. Our digital footprint is used to track our devices and what we do online.

There are two types of digital footprints, which include active and passive digital footprints.

Active digital footprints involve us deliberately sharing our online activity. Think of when you make a social media post. You're sharing information while alerting everyone that you were online at a specific time. Simultaneously, when you enter a digital platform with a registered username and password, you create a digital footprint. Other forms of actively sharing your digital footprint are when you accept cookies, complete an online form or survey, subscribe to a newsletter, and more.

On the other hand, passive digital footprints are created when we are unaware that our data is being taken. This can happen when the websites we use track how many times we use the website, how long we stay, take our IP addresses, and more. Other places that also tend to track our digital footprint are social media sites. They look into what we like, which posts we lingered on the longest, which ads we liked, and more. The idea is to continue to give you the content you enjoy, thus personalizing your feed.

We may be asking ourselves why our digital footprint matters and the impact it may have on our daily lives. Well, the answer is simple: our digital footprints are relatively permanent. Have you ever had someone tell you that once something is on the internet, it's on it forever? This is because our digital footprints can be shared with the public and, once this is done, we have little to no control over what happens next.

Another major reason is that our digital footprint impacts our digital reputation. Our digital reputation can affect our real-life reputation because, just as we are what we eat, we are what we post, like, and share.

Did you know that your digital footprint could also affect your job opportunities? More employers are seeking to know more about their employees or potential employees. They turn to social media in the hope that they can gain a better understanding of who you are as a person. This means that if you post anything that goes against their company policies, you could find yourself searching for another job.

For this reason, you'll want to be careful of the pictures, posts, and information you share. Sometimes, we may find that private conversations, images, and videos have been leaked to the public. This could also potentially harm our digital footprint.

In recent times, we've seen more and more people fall prey to cyber criminals who are seeking to exploit your digital footprint. They can use this information for phishing or to create a false identity using your data.

Overcoming issues with your digital footprint could include being cautious of the websites you visit and being careful of the things you post. You can also do things like avoid oversharing on social media, avoid websites you may believe are unsafe, avoid using public WiFi, keep your software up-to-date, and more.

Balancing Offline and Online Interactions

A major issue that comes with the digital dimension is trying to strike a balance between offline and online interactions. Communication has changed from written letters, phone calls, and gatherings to messages, images, and videos on social media platforms. Although online platforms have made it easier for us to communicate from anywhere in the world, they also take away from the richness of communication and social interaction. In this section, we explore the digital dimension and how to find a balance between real-life interaction and social media.

Blending Real World and Digital Interaction

People who use technology to keep in touch usually fall under two categories, which include those who use social media to enhance their real-life interactions and those who replace real-life interaction with social media. Both are using social media; however, they have different understandings of what social media is meant for.

Social media and other communication platforms were meant to enhance our ability to communicate with those we love. It offers us the chance to interact with those we love even when we aren't in their midst; however, it is not a substitute for interaction. Some may argue that social platforms have afforded us the chance to interact with a larger and more specific group of people. Although this is true, some benefits come with real-life interactions that we've already covered.

Emoticons and Emotions

Emoticons, also known as emojis, were meant to help bridge the gap between emotion and text. They were meant to offer the effect of non-verbal cues; however, they fall short of expressing the truth about how we may be feeling.

When we have in-person or phone call conversations we're able to add context to the words. We can listen to the tone of their voice and the subtle hints from the way they do things. We can hear when their voice breaks in pain, joy, or excitement.

Unfortunately, the luxury of always being available for a call isn't always an option. In today's world, where independence is key and the cost of living is rising, it makes it difficult for us to keep in touch through phone calls or meet-ups. The only solution seems to be social platforms, which means that finding a balance is a must.

Integrating Social Media and Real-Life Interaction

Over the years, the line between real-life interaction and social media has been blurred, and sometimes we no longer see it. Connecting through social media and maintaining relationships, friendships, family ties, and more on social media has become the order of the day. The more time we spend on social media platforms, the less time we have real-life interaction, causing us to replace real-life interaction with social media. So, how do we find the balance between them?

Well, the answer lies in creating connections in real life and using social media to maintain communication. In other words, we can use social media to nurture our relationships.

One of the many things that can also assist in keeping us in touch with reality is setting limits on how much time we're willing to spend on social media. Setting time limits can stop us from spending hours on social media platforms. Instead, we can use the time we would have spent on social media cultivating real-life relationships or doing something we enjoy.

Adjusting your life may seem difficult; however, it is necessary to ensure that we increase our quality of life. The more we connect with people, the happier we may become.

Virtual Communication Skills

Virtual communication can be described and defined as the use of digital means to facilitate communication between people. These digital means can come in the form of text messages, chats, emails, and more. In Chapter 2, we took a look at communication from a physical point; however, exploring the digital dimension requires that we take a deeper look into virtual communication.

Effective Communication in The Digital Age

Effective communication can be described as our ability to convey a message in a manner that can be understood by the receiver. To effectively communicate using digital platforms we can utilize the following approaches.

Be Clear and Concise

Over the years, our attention spans have decreased, meaning that we are unable to concentrate for extended periods of time. To combat this and ensure that your message is received in the manner you need, you'll need to ensure that your message is clear, concise, and well thought out. The approach for a digital message should be less is more.

Try Active Listening

It may sound a little out of place; however, active listening plays a major role in our ability to effectively communicate especially in the digital space. When you're actively listening and paying attention, you can ask questions to clarify certain sections you're not sure of. This shows genuine interest and can help strengthen the connection while also building trust.

Pay Attention to Non-Verbal Cues

We're constantly sending subtle messages that help the receiver develop an idea of what we mean. In the digital space, non-verbal cues can be emojis, writing style, and tone, and during video calls, it can be certain mannerisms. The idea is to read your message through a fresh pair of eyes to ensure that it conveys what it needs to.

Emotional Intelligence and Empathy

In a previous chapter, we spoke about how technology may harm empathy. This is because we cannot see or read into the emotions of others through text meaning that the emotions behind the message are not conveyed. Exercising empathy can play a vital role in digital communication as it shows the next person that we understand their frustrations and sympathize with their circumstances. Showing empathy while using emotional intelligence can help us build stronger relationships, resolve conflict quicker, and shift the culture of the digital spaces we occupy.

Trust

A key component in communication of any kind is trust. When we trust one another, we're able to see a message for what it is and not what we deem it to be. We can build trust by being authentic, reliable, following through on our actions, being respectful of time and opinions, and more.

Improvement

Always keep in mind that we can improve our communication skills. Doing little things such as asking for feedback or learning from experience are an amazing way to improve your communication skills. Thankfully, with the use of technology, we can find better and different ways to communicate.

Effective communication in the digital space is possible especially when we are set on ensuring that we communicate well. By abiding by digital etiquette, we can find better and more effective ways to communicate.

The Nuances of Digital Etiquette

Digital etiquette, also known as netiquette, can be defined as the customs or rules that define how we can behave in the digital space. It provides a moral compass on what is right and wrong while also defining the lines of what can be considered bullying or inappropriate behavior.

We can exercise digital etiquette by:

Being Respectful

At times, we tend to forget that the people we are engaging with online are real human beings who have feelings. By being respectful, we can think about what we're about to post and how it could affect others.

Being respectful simply means that we do not post or comment on things that could be classified as rude or mean. Instead, when needing to comment, we do so without offending the people who may come across our post or comment.

When making a post or planning to comment, it's always best to think twice about how the message will be received. Oftentimes, the banter we think will be funny is not and can cause others to feel uncomfortable or hurt.

Be Careful of Plagiarism

In today's age, plagiarism has turned into a serious problem because many of us do not credit the creators of our content. Doing simple things such as tagging or quoting an author can help combat plagiarism and give credit to those who come up with ideas.

Check Your Grammar

One of the many ways that a message can be misunderstood is by using poor grammar or punctuation. Simple mistakes, especially in English, can lead to major issues so you'll always want to ensure that you are checking your grammar, messages, and punctuation for any mistakes. You can also use free grammar checkers such as Grammarly, Quilbot, and more.

Additionally, be mindful of how you type messages. Sending a message in all capital letters can be construed as shouting, which can alter the intention of the message.

Ask For Permission

The internet is so fast-paced that we may find ourselves falling into giving out personal information in the hopes that the next person won't mind. When wanting to share personal information, you'll always want to make sure that you obtain permission.

Silence Your Devices

Our smartphones can be seen as distractions especially when we're trying to engage with others. Try your best to remain off your phone while also letting those you speak to know that you have something to attend to. This way there is no confusion on either side about what you're doing and why.

The intricacies of digital etiquette, when broken down, are simple and can be executed by many of us. The idea is to maintain peace and offer all users the freedom to speak within certain boundaries. For this reason, many social media platforms have altered their guidelines to ensure that all are as safe as possible. Although there's still a long way, there has also been a lot of headway made.

Maintaining Authenticity and Honesty Online

When on social media, it is easy to get swept away by the lives and achievements of others because the order of the day is perfection. Although this is true, maintaining authenticity and honesty online is vital. So, what is authenticity in the context of social media?

Authenticity is simply about remaining true to yourself, your values, and your beliefs. It's about showing the reality of who you are and the things that you hold dear to your heart. Maintaining authenticity requires transparency, honesty, and the ability to be vulnerable with those on your platform.

When we are authentic, we're able to create real connections with those who follow us. This affords them the chance to interact with us from a more personal point. It also offers us a sense of humanity and realism in a world that only sees perfection. The more we share our realities, the more we can engage and inspire those around us. We can also create real support groups while showing others that their lives and experiences matter.

How to be Authentic and Honest on Social Media

For many of us, the process and maintenance of honesty and authenticity is something we are unfamiliar with. We are scared of sharing the intimate parts of ourselves due to fear. So, how do we maintain and become honest?

Share Your Story

Your journey to maintaining your authenticity starts with you sharing and being true to your story. Who we are as people is what creates our story, and by sharing our experiences, we can help maintain and create authenticity. This can be something as small as sharing our art, gifts, and talents. There is always room for your art, even if you believe that there isn't.

Transparency

Part of being authentic is to remain as transparent as possible. This means sharing failures, happy moments, and more. The idea is to ensure that you are as honest as possible on your social media platforms.

Post What Is True

When posting on social media, you'll want to only post what is true. This means doing your research before sharing any posts. It also means posting current pictures and sharing information about yourself that is true.

Taking a step toward authenticity can seem daunting; however, it is necessary especially when trying to build something solid. The digital dimension has made many changes to who we are as people and the voices we use to express our messages. Reverting to authenticity can help us reset and work on personal values.

NAVIGATING CHALLENGES IN RELATIONSHIPS

Conflict Resolution

Our ability to resolve conflict plays a major role in our ability to build and maintain social relationships. In this section, we take a deeper look into conflict resolution by understanding its common causes, how we can resolve it effectively, and the importance of forgiveness and letting go.

Understanding Common Sources of Conflict

To understand the common causes of conflict, we first need to understand what conflict is. Conflict can be described as a struggle or clash that occurs between two forces. Usually, the situation is marked by the forces being unable to agree on something, which disrupts harmony.

There are five main reasons why we may find ourselves engaging in conflict. These five include:

Information Conflict

Have you ever engaged in an argument with someone only to find that either they or you were misinformed? Information conflict arises when we are unable to agree on the data involving the situation. It's either we are misinformed or do not have sufficient information to engage in the conversation.

Usually, the parties involved would want to look at each other's information while simultaneously researching the points of the other party. Unfortunately, this is not always the case, especially in social relationships.

Value Conflicts

Our values, morals, and beliefs play a major role in who we are as people and the way that we function in the world. Value conflicts arise when we have perceived or incompatible belief systems.

Conflict within this area only arises when we deem our beliefs as the only beliefs that should be followed. At this point, we begin to impose our beliefs on others, which causes conflict, as they may have their own belief and value systems.

Interests Conflicts

One of the many causes of conflict is different interests, which results in interests conflict. Common causes of this type of conflict can be money, resources, and or time. The idea is that our interest is more important than that of other persons. This can cause people to feel as though they are not important, which may result in issues.

Relationship Conflicts

For many of us, conflict within our relationships is something we experience regularly. Relationship conflicts arise due to issues with perception, negative emotions, or poor communication. This usually happens when we are unable to trust in the intentions of one another, causing us to feel unsafe emotionally. For many, this could be a trigger that stems from past trauma.

Structural Conflicts

Structural conflicts are usually caused by oppressive behaviors. This means that we may be on the receiving end of limited resources and opportunities. This can cause us to feel frustrated and want or need to voice our opinion, meaning that conflict will arise.

Conflict arises when there are issues with agreement between parties. To build and maintain social relationships, we need to understand how we should be handling conflict and the different things we can do when conflict arises.

Strategies For Effective Conflict Resolution

Now that we understand the five most common causes of conflict, we can look into the different strategies we can use to resolve them. As people, we may have already come up with our strategies for conflict resolution that may include avoidance, accommodating, compromising, defeating, and collaborating. These strategies are usually put into place based on how cooperative or assertive we want to be during the process of conflict resolution. By understanding these methods, we can help to resolve conflict more effectively.

Avoidance

For some people, avoiding the conflict as a whole seems better than engaging in it, especially when they feel that they won't gain anything by being vocal. Unfortunately, this method does not help to resolve conflict but can exacerbate the situation, causing us to become resentful, angry, and hurt. When we hold on to these feelings, we may start other arguments.

Competing

When we compete, our main focus is to win and not necessarily to resolve the conflict. The idea behind this type of conflict resolution is that everyone else is wrong while we are right. By using this tactic, we are assertive; however, we refuse to listen to the opinions of others, causing us to be misinformed and unable to listen.

Accommodation

For many of us, this tends to be the solution when we feel as though we are wrong. Although this is seen as a healthy form of conflict resolution, it is not, as both parties need to accommodate the other. One sided accommodation can lead to issues with anger, resentment, and hurt, which can harm the relationship as a whole.

Collaboration

A great way to solve conflict is to collaborate. This means that all parties are afforded the chance to voice their opinion and perspectives. Once all parties have spoken, a solution is then brought forward and implemented. This option of conflict resolution affords everyone the chance to be both assertive and cooperative.

Compromise

The idea behind this form of conflict resolution is that we all get a little bit of what we want. We're able to voice our opinions while sharing our concerns; this means that we are both assertive and cooperative. When we think of this type of conflict resolution, we think of fairness, which may not always be the case. Ideally, compromise requires that we consider the voice of everyone while offering a solution that can work for everyone involved, but sometimes one side benefits more than the others.

How to Properly Handle and Deal With Conflict

Now that we know the different strategies we may use to deal with conflict, we can focus on how we can properly handle and deal with conflict.

Respect Boundaries

In Chapter 2, we discussed boundaries and how we should put them into place. Using this information, we can effectively navigate through conflict. Boundaries are meant to help us not cross the line and act as a type of moral compass for ourselves and others.

During conflict resolution, lines may become blurred; however, we need to ensure we maintain our own and the other parties' boundaries. This is because crossing boundaries can worsen conflict and make things extremely uncomfortable for all.

Find the Real Issue

In the previous section, we took a look at the top five reasons for conflict issues. During the process of conflict resolution, it's always best to look into what the real issue may be. Oftentimes, the issue can be resolved through conversation, reassurance, a behavior change, and more. When we deal with the real issue, we're able to move forward in a manner that makes sense to everyone.

This part of conflict resolution requires that we listen with active listening skills. Additionally, we may need to use empathy to fully understand the next person's argument.

Compromise

A huge part of social relationships is compromise. This shows our circle that we are willing to work with them and that they are important to us. We can only reach a point of compromise through listening and consideration.

Conflict resolution looks different for everyone, which is why it is not a one-size-fits-all scenario. The important thing is to ensure that those we engage in conflict with know that we hear their truth even while pushing our own. Do your best to remember that it isn't about who wins the argument but rather that healthy resolutions are made. If need be, take the time to rethink the issues at hand and come back when you're in a better state. Ensure that you do this as soon as possible to avoid feelings of resentment and anger.

Conflict resolution requires that we forgive, and in the next section, we will tackle how you can start the process of forgiveness and letting go.

The Importance of Forgiveness and Letting Go

> *We must develop and maintain the capacity to forgive. He who is devoid of the power to forgive is devoid of the power to love.* –Martin Luther King Jr.

Our ability to forgive those who have hurt us plays a major role in our social relationships. Unforgiveness can be described as a state of emotional or mental distress caused by our inability or unwillingness to let go of resentment, anger, and hurt toward a certain situation.

When we are unwilling to forgive we may experience stress, depression, anxiety, social isolation, or a compromised immune system. Unforgiveness keeps the pain and misery of that situation alive, which can cause us to become bitter. This can affect our thought patterns and turn us into pessimistic individuals.

Dealing With Unforgiveness

There is power in freeing ourselves from things that no longer serve us. Harboring unforgiveness can do us more harm than good and can lead us down a very steep and ugly path. Although forgiveness comes naturally to some, it does not mean that we cannot learn how to forgive.

Forgiveness does not mean that we excuse the action that inflicted pain, but rather that we are no longer allowing that pain and person to continue to hurt us. Additionally, forgiveness does not mean that we need to keep in contact with or continue a relationship with an individual we know is toxic or does not positively contribute to our lives. It simply means letting go of the situation and focusing on healing.

Various benefits come with forgiveness, which include things such as improved mental health, healthier and better relationships, a decrease in anxiety and stress, a stronger immune system, improved health and self-esteem, and more. When we forgive, we commit to change, which will need practice. We can start the process of forgiveness by:

- Recognizing the power of forgiveness and the impact it may have on our lives
- Identifying the situation that needs healing and the person who hurt us
- Acknowledging how the situation made us feel and admitting how this action changed our lives
- Releasing the emotions associated with the situation and person
- Joining a support group that specializes in what we've gone through or going to therapy or counseling
- Forgiving the person who has harmed us

Unfortunately, forgiveness isn't always easy, especially when the wound inflicted cuts deep. For many of us, holding onto the grudge is far less work than having to deal with the pain inflicted. If you're still struggling with forgiveness, you can:

- Practice empathy by placing yourself in their shoes and trying to see things from their perspective.
- Reflect on instances where you were the offender and needed forgiveness.
- Learn that sometimes we may need help along the way of our healing journey. Sometimes doing things such as journaling, praying, or participating in guided meditation can help to release unforgiveness.
- Be gentle with yourself and let go of unforgiveness. Forgiveness is an intense process that can take a long time to do, so be gentle with yourself.

Many times, especially when it comes to forgiveness, we may find ourselves struggling to forgive ourselves. This can be a result of something we did or our inability to act when the act was being committed. When navigating self forgiveness, you'll want to be as honest with yourself as possible and avoid judging yourself too harshly. Ask for forgiveness, even if you're simply asking yourself. Acknowledge that what you have done has caused pain and that you are no longer willing to continue in that direction.

When we work on ourselves, we work on the versions of ourselves that have been left behind and hurt. The better we become, the less toxic we are for others, and the healthier we become.

Dealing With Toxic Relationships

Toxic relationships can be defined as human bonds or ties with unhealthy dynamics that can cause distress or harm. As a result, we may feel manipulated, disrespected, and unsupported, causing us to feel unloved, unseen, and unappreciated.

A truly toxic relationship is characterized by the give-and-take dynamic. This means that one party is taking while the other is constantly giving. This means that the relationship is based on your ability to constantly give while they never offer anything.

For many, the discussion centered around toxic relationships is shortly followed by abusive relationships. Keep in mind that toxic relationships can become abusive and that all abusive relationships are toxic.

No one deserves to be in an abusive relationship, and if you or someone you know is currently being abused, it's always best to get help for them sooner rather than later. If you need assistance, try going to your local police station, which can link you to the resources you need.

Identifying Signs of a Toxic Relationship

Identifying a toxic relationship can be difficult, especially when we're still trying to distinguish what's truly going on. Here are a few signs that you or someone you know may be in a toxic relationship.

Every relationship requires that there be a certain level of emotional safety. Emotional safety simply means that we can share our feelings and thoughts without being shamed or feeling as though how we feel doesn't matter.

In a healthy relationship dynamic, we're able to share feelings and thoughts without fear of judgment or hurt. Keep in mind that emotional safety has its limits and that it isn't everyone whom you can share your deepest thoughts and pain with.

Communication Is Poor or Non-Existent

Communication is a fundamental part of any relationship. It helps us convey a message about how we may feel, which is why it's so important. Toxic relationships lead us to bury our emotions within ourselves, causing us to become resentful, angry, or hurt. This is because, when we express our emotions and needs, we're met with dishonesty, manipulation, gaslighting, or judgment.

Exploitation and Neglect

Nurturing is an amazing way to care for our partners as it lets them know that we care about them. When we neglect our partner's needs, we show them that we are no longer interested in the relationship. A toxic relationship is characterized by exploitation and neglect because your basic needs are not being met.

Lack of Autonomy

We tend to lose ourselves in toxic relationships. This is because we're constantly having to mold ourselves to fit the needs of our partner, meaning that we no longer do what we used to. Instead, we may find ourselves unable to say no for fear of the emotional manipulation that comes afterward.

Judgment

Toxic relationships are comprised of a lot of judgment, especially when we make mistakes. We may also be judged on our past or past mistakes making it hard to function in the relationship.

As human beings, making mistakes is part of life, meaning that we should be more compassionate toward ourselves and others. In toxic relationships, compassion and empathy are replaced with judgment.

Feeling Belittled

A lack of emotional maturity can push toxic partners to belittle us. When people are emotionally immature, they use our wrongdoings, mistakes, or past ventures to belittle us and cause us to feel small.

Dysfunction

Oftentimes, toxicity is characterized by dysfunctional roles. This simply means that we place others' needs over ours while constantly working to fix or nurture them. In many instances, we are forced into this role as the toxic partner refuses to contribute toward the relationship. Not only is this draining, it is also hurtful, as we may end up questioning our self-worth.

Manipulation

Control or manipulation are tactics used by a toxic individual to try and maintain power within the relationship. They may weaponize the relationship to try and get what they want from you such as staying in or giving up a friendship. Isolation is a classic tactic used by toxic individuals. Someone who loves you will allow you to be in a relationship with them and still maintain your old life.

Another well-known form of manipulation or control is the use of rage. Toxic individuals may be chronically angry making it difficult for them to exist in the relationship. You may find yourself constantly having to hide making it difficult for you to express yourself.

Jealousy

Major jealousy issues can be signs of a toxic relationship. Oftentimes, there will be jealousy over some of the simple activities such as going to the gym or having friendships of the opposite sex. Excessive jealousy can lead to issues with rage and a constant need for you to be by their side.

For many of us, dealing with a toxic partner is something we may find difficult. In the next section, we cover different strategies that can help you handle or deal with a toxic person.

Strategies for Handling Toxic Individuals

Handling a toxic person can be difficult especially when we love them or they are in power positions. Below we offer a few strategies that can help you handle toxic individuals.

Maintain Your Boundaries

Toxic individuals may constantly feel the need to violate our boundaries no matter how many times we've communicated them. The idea is to continue to assert their power over you, making you feel helpless. In the midst of this, we must remain as assertive as possible while enforcing our boundaries. Enforcing boundaries can start with a lot of guilt, especially when they begin to make certain comments; however, standing your ground and ensuring that you work on feelings of guilt is vital. Over time, you will no longer feel guilty for your boundaries and the needs you have and continue to vocalize.

Avoid the Drama

For many of us, our curiosity tends to get the better of us when it comes to bad news. Toxic individuals are constantly involved in some form of drama. When this happens, you'll want to distance yourself as soon as possible to avoid getting in the mix. If you can't avoid the drama, then try your best to engage as little as possible even if you have the right solution.

Attempting to fix the situation could lead you into an endless cycle of discussions that have no solution. This can become draining and emotionally taxing.

Try Talking to Them

Many toxic individuals are unaware of how their behavior affects you. By sitting them down and speaking about how their behavior or words make you feel, you make them aware. Some may resort to apologizing, while others may make you feel as though you are taking things a little too personally. Either way, communicating your feelings is important and can lead to some form of improvement.

Keep in mind that some toxic people may have things such as a mental illness or personality disorders that will make getting your message across difficult. If this is the case, you'll want them to seek professional assistance.

Limit Your Time

Unfortunately, when dealing with toxic individuals, you'll want to try your best to limit your time with them. This means making minimal contact and doing your best to keep to yourself.

Toxic individuals will always find a way to place the blame on someone else. This brings on feelings of guilt, which can worsen the situation. To help yourself, try your best to ditch all forms of guilt and shame. This can stop the psychological issues that come with dealing with a toxic individual.

Dealing with toxic individuals can become traumatic, which is why you may need to seek professional help. This will help mend or heal any trauma that you may have experienced while being in contact with them.

When and How to End a Toxic Relationship

Ending a toxic relationship can be hard; however, it is necessary. In this section, we explore when and how you can end your toxic relationship. So, how do we end toxic relationships?

Issues With Respect

Relationships are about reciprocation, especially when it comes to respect. Toxic individuals may request that you respect them and their wishes even though they are not willing to do the same for you. A good time to leave is when your boundaries are being disrespected or you are being purposefully humiliated and disrespected by them.

Disrespect can also extend to your ability to do things on your own. You may find that they exert control through your finances, clothing, hobbies, personal endeavors, and personal space. The idea is to keep you as close as possible while simultaneously breaking you down. This is a form of abuse and should not be taken lightly.

A General Lack of Happiness

Although our relationships should not be responsible for our happiness, they can be responsible for our misery. Common signs of a toxic relationship include mental and emotional exhaustion from problems that aren't being solved, along with poor communication and control.

For many of us, admitting that our partner is the issue is not something we enjoy. We may find ourselves coming up with other reasons as to why we are experiencing issues; however, upon closer inspection, we may find that our partners are the source of our issues.

When You Turn Into Someone Else

Toxic relationships tend to bring out the worst in us, and, if we stay in them long enough, we lose who are. If you look in the mirror and struggle to recognize who you've turned into, it's a good time to leave. Relationships are meant to foster positive growth and change.

Co-Dependency

A huge sign that you're in a toxic relationship is co-dependency. This is where one or both parties rely on each other and become enablers for toxic behaviors. If you experience any of these signs it's always a good time to leave:

- lack of self-esteem
- inability to make choices on your own
- struggle with recognizing your feelings
- you lack personal time and are anxious when you are apart
- have issues with establishing boundaries

Taking stock of our relationships can help us know when it's time to leave. Leaving is never an easy decision, but it is necessary to save yourself.

Now that we understand when you need to leave a toxic relationship, we can focus on how you can leave. Leaving such situations is always tough, especially when you don't know how. Below we explore the different things you can do to leave your toxic relationship.

Build a Safety Net

Leaving a toxic relationship requires that you have a plan of action. Think of everything you'll need to overcome certain aspects of the separation. Do you need a place to stay? Where will you get the money?

Oftentimes, toxic individuals target people who cannot find their way out. During the relationship, they may pressure you into sharing finances, moving in with them, and more. For this reason, you'll want to think of your independence and how you'll get it back.

Speak to Someone

Being in a toxic relationship can make you feel embarrassed, even though there is nothing to be ashamed of. Alert a family member or friend about your intentions of leaving so that they know what's going on.

During this time, you may want to seek out professional help to assist you with freeing yourself mentally while also assisting you to overcome the trauma.

Go No-Contact

Struggles with communication may arise when you are dealing with a toxic partner. They may promise things such as change or going to counseling, but they are simply trying to lure you back. By going no-contact, you can ensure that you leave the relationship fully.

Leaving toxic relationships requires that we heal. In the next section, we focus on how you can start the process of healing after a toxic relationship.

Healing From the Aftermath of a Toxic Relationship

The moment you realize you deserve better, everything will change. –Unknown

Getting out of a toxic relationship is hard, but taking the first few steps toward healing is even harder. This is because toxic relationships take a massive toll on our mental and physical health due to the behaviors we were exposed to, such as manipulation, control, belittling, and criticism. All of these can lead us toward issues such as anxiety, depression, and low self-esteem.

Depending on the duration and severity of the toxic relationship, you may find yourself experiencing many emotions at once, causing you to believe that you may lack emotional clarity. This can have a massive impact on our ability to reason and see the healing process through. So, how do we deal with the aftermath of a toxic relationship?

Go No-Contact

Healing cannot take place in the same environment where the pain was inflicted. Moving forward from a toxic relationship may require that we sever all forms of contact including emails, messaging, phone calls, and any other platform where the toxic individual may have access to you.

If contact is necessary, you may want to ensure that you involve a third party to help you navigate communication. This may seem tedious; however, it is necessary.

Reconnect With the Emotionally Healthy

Reconnecting with people you once trusted is an amazing way to start the process of healing. In many cases, toxic individuals cut us off from healthy individuals so that they can continue to be toxic. By reconnecting with those we once knew, we reconnect with our old selves, which can help us along the journey of healing.

Do Not Seek Closure

We tend to seek closure or a reason behind why we were on the receiving end of toxicity. Unfortunately, these answers or apologies may never come because toxic individuals rarely take accountability for their actions. We may also be seeking closure because we cannot accept that we allowed ourselves into that situation. Acceptance and forgiveness can help us look past our mistakes and offer us the closure of knowing that we did nothing wrong.

Seek a Mental Health Professional

Sometimes we may feel like those around us do not understand what we've been through and what we're dealing with. Contacting a trained professional who specializes in mental health can help you process the feelings and thoughts of the toxic relationship. They can also come up with a tailored plan to help you get back into the swing of things.

Journaling

At times, we underestimate the power of writing down our thoughts and experiences. Writing can offer us the chance to process our thoughts clearly and help us understand what is truly going on and how we feel about a matter. It can also help us gain clarity on certain events and things that were said.

Dealing with the aftermath of a toxic relationship can take years. We may find ourselves being triggered or suffering from things such as PTSD. Healing is a process that requires us to take things slowly and embrace the idea of a new life and a second chance. Doing things such as volunteering in shelters can help us get into contact with people who share similar experiences, affording us the chance to build a community. Finding purpose in the pain can help to alleviate feelings of low self-worth that may have been picked up in the toxic relationship.

The Art of Letting Go

The art of letting go is a process or system that involves detaching from things that no longer serve us or cause us some form of misery or harm. We can let go of things such as toxic relationships, situations, family bonds or ties, and more.

Recognizing When a Relationship Is No Longer Beneficial

For many of us, when we get into relationships, we plan on staying in them. Unfortunately, this isn't always the case, as things can happen along the way that cause us to question our capability for staying in the relationship. For some, knowing when to leave a relationship is problematic, especially when they see the issues they are facing as small. In this section, we explore the signs that your relationship may no longer be beneficial.

Lack of Communication

When we think of communication, we're usually thinking of light conversation. Relationships are made up of layers of communication which can help to ensure that we remain emotionally safe to share our feelings and needs. A lack of communication due to fear of causing conflict is a major red flag and can be grounds to end your relationship as a whole.

Issues With Compromise or Sacrifice

Compromise and sacrifice are vital in a relationship. This is because no two people have the same interests and needs. When we compromise or sacrifice, we show the other person that we care. A refusal to do so can mean that your partner is no longer interested in the relationship or that they weigh their own needs above your own. This imbalance can cause issues and force one partner into always sacrificing.

Lack of Support

Support is always appreciated in every relationship and makes us feel as though we matter. If your partner is no longer willing to support your endeavors, then it's always a good time to walk away.

Constant Apologies

Have you ever been in a situation where no matter what you did or said you were always wrong? Being in a state of constantly having to apologize is one of the many signs that the relationship is toxic and needs to end.

During this time, you may feel as though your boundaries are being disrespected and that you are no longer of value.

Controlling Behavior

When our autonomy is no longer on the table, it's a good sign to leave. Controlling behavior could be restricting your movement, your ability to text others, and more.

Abusive behaviors are also a good sign to leave. If you're struggling to end a relationship, ask for a second or third opinion to help you figure out if your relationship is healthy and worth saving. Toxicity can cause us to live an unhappy life, and we are all deserving of happiness and joy.

Coping With the Loss of a Relationship

Loss in all forms is tragic, including that of a relationship you hoped would make it. Finding a way to cope with loss is something we may struggle with. So, how do we cope with loss?

Allow Yourself to Grieve

Grief is something many of us tend to run away from because it puts us in a vulnerable position. We become extremely emotional because in relationships we grieve more than one loss. We're also grieving shared memories and companionship while also grieving the loss of support, hopes, dreams, and plans. In certain moments, the grief may become greater than we can bear as the emotions we are going through intensify.

Allowing yourself to grieve is part of the healing process. It may seem like an endless abyss of pain, but things will not remain this way forever. Think of grief as a sign that you once loved and could love; it is a mark of possibility.

Reach Out for Support

Support can play a major role in our ability to overcome grief or loss. When we have support, we're able to reach for assistance when necessary. Isolation can magnify feelings of hurt and pain and the overall experience, causing us to believe that this is a never-ending process.

Not all of us experience support the same way, so it's always best to communicate your support needs with family and friends who support you.

Take Care of Yourself

Loss can cause us to lose touch with looking after ourselves because we're focused on the grief. Even though we may not feel up to it, we must look after ourselves and our mental, emotional, and physical well-being.

Taking care of yourself can come in many forms, such as going to see a therapist, writing in a journal, praying, painting, or even walking. Find out what taking care of yourself means to you and use this as an opportunity to relearn yourself and your new identity.

Coping with the loss of a relationship can prove difficult, especially when there are feelings that remain. Although this is true, moving on is necessary and can help give you a new identity and a second chance at life.

Learning From Relationship Endings

Learning sometimes happens in or during failure, especially when it comes to relationships. This means that there is something we can learn from every unsuccessful venture in our life, including a loss.

To learn from your previous relationship, you need to ask yourself five important questions. These questions may lead to other questions and can start your process of learning more about yourself.

1. Taking a step back and looking at your relationship as a whole, how do you believe you contributed toward its demise?

2. Are you constantly choosing different partners with the same character traits? If so, where do you believe this behavior and choice stems from?

3. Consider your behavior and how you handle conflict: do you handle conflict, stress, and insecurities constructively? Where did you adopt these behaviors and do you believe they are healthy?

4. Do you choose potential over patterns with your partners? What do you believe are the causes of your doing so? Think back to your parents or your guardians and how they behaved toward you. Additionally, you may want to think of where you saw and experienced love between two adults. What was that experience like, and do you think that those relationships were healthy?

5. How do you handle your feelings when you are upset, hurt, or disappointed? Are you emotionally disciplined or do your feelings and emotions rule over you?

As human beings, it is our responsibility to seek out why we may be behaving in a certain way. Oftentimes, we do not realize how wounded we are until there are situations of pain that cause us to reflect. These are perfect moments to learn and adjust if we allow them and recognize them as such.

CULTIVATING PROFESSIONAL RELATIONSHIPS

The Importance of Networking in Career Development

A network can be defined as a link between two or more computers to share resources such as exchange electronic files, printers, CDs, and USBs. The computers operating on the network can be linked together via cables, satellites, radio waves, telephone lines, and infrared light beams.

The same can be said for social networks. A social network can be defined as a group of people that share specific interests or professions. Their main goal is to share information and opportunities to help further their interests or careers.

Identifying and Creating Networking Opportunities

Have you ever heard someone refer to your network as your net worth? This is because innovation, collaboration, and opportunity can be found in the circles we run in. The simple act of networking can turn into amazing opportunities, especially in terms of career management. The key to yielding favorable results during the networking process is to find the right network. So, how do we identify and create new networking opportunities?

Conduct a SWOT Analysis

A SWOT analysis is usually conducted in business when an organization wants to thrive. They take stock of their strengths, weaknesses, opportunities, and threats to get an edge in the market. Think of creating your network the same way you would a SWOT analysis. Take stock of strengths, weaknesses, opportunities, and threats within your network and the different things you could use your network for when it comes to career advancements. Keep in mind that this technique is done before you make any changes to your network.

Define Your Objectives

To network effectively, you'll need to look into your career goals and objectives. What exactly are you hoping to achieve through this network and why? By asking ourselves these questions, we can avoid pursuing things that will not yield any results.

Look for Opportunity

After having defined your networking goals, you'll want to do your research and look for networking opportunities that match what you're looking for. When conducting research, you can use any sources including social media platforms, referrals, emails, and more. You'll want to be careful of the opportunities you select and will want to choose based on relevance, accessibility to events, and more.

Have Network Interactions

Now that you sought networking opportunities, it's time to engage with your network but not before some preparation. Create an introduction that is clear and concise about who you are, what you do, and the values you have to offer. Prepare a few questions that allow for conversation which can help to make the interaction memorable. After this interaction, be sure to follow up on the lead.

Check Your Results

It's always a good idea to check whether or not our networking strategy is working. You can do this by looking at the quality and quantity of your interactions while also looking at the outcome of your strategy. Something to also look into is your networking skills and what seemed to work and what didn't. When we evaluate our skills and overall strategy, we create room for improvement.

Working on and creating a network of like-minded individuals may be hard. We'll constantly need to refine our strategies and work on finding the best spaces to infiltrate. The idea is to build meaningful connections that can yield results.

Building Meaningful Connections in Professional Settings

Creating meaningful connections is one of the best ways to advance your career, meaning that it is essential for you to network. Meaningful connections could lead to collaboration and career insights and information that push the boundaries of your career. You can start building meaningful connections in professional settings by:

Attend the Right Industry Events

We cannot find what we're looking for by being in the wrong place. Industry events, both virtual and in-person, are fantastic places to create connections. They offer you the chance to be with like-minded people who share similar goals. This would be the perfect time to network and gather contact information.

Join the Right Associations or Communities

Joining the right association or community affords us the chance to build our network. When doing this, you'll want to look at whether the objectives and goals of the page or association align with your professional goals and objectives. If it's a page, take a look at the engagement, posts, and comments to get a feel of what the page is like. Usually, in these spaces, your ideas and contributions will be highly appreciated.

During this time, you'll want to look into professional pages that can easily connect you with like-minded people. Platforms such as LinkedIn can offer you opportunities for networking with some providing this free of charge.

Make Time to Build

Although it may seem obvious, we must allocate time to build our professional network. During this time, we can seek out events, pages, and other things that align with our professional goals and objectives. When we allocate time, we ensure that building becomes an integral part of our professional routine.

When building professional relationships, you'll want to:

- remain authentic
- practice active listening while asking thoughtful questions
- nurture your relationships through follow-ups
- and remain and be as helpful as possible

Connecting with people, especially in professional spaces, isn't always something that comes naturally. Although we may want to shy away from building connections, we need to continue to push toward building our network.

Networking Etiquette and Follow-up Strategies

The way we carry ourselves is vital, especially when we're trying to form new bonds. This is because, upon first encounters, people tend to assume who we are and the things we stand for based on appearance and the way we carry ourselves.

When we refer to etiquette, we're simply referring to a set of rules that govern the way we interact and behave. As we enter spaces or fields, we'll want to learn more about etiquette to create a good first impression. Below we offer you a few network etiquette rules that can help you in your follow-up strategies.

Be Respectful

Being respectful and courteous plays a major role in our ability to create connections. In a previous chapter, we spoke about diversity, what it is, and why it's important. The professional space is full of diverse individuals, meaning that during our time, we'll need to be respectful of different views and opinions. While these are being shared, you'll want to allow everyone the chance to speak. Do not try to dominate the conversation as this may not be well received.

Be Authentic

Creating authentic connections is about being as authentic and genuine as possible. This means avoiding tactics of manipulation or flattery to get what you want. The idea is to create connections that last and afford you the chance to grow, which can only be achieved through common interests and shared values and experiences which are slightly more personal.

Be Proactive

To network we need to prepare and be proactive. Preparation includes things such as thinking of an appropriate approach, coming up with a strategy or template for emails and messages, and setting your goals for interactions. This can make interactions far more comfortable and offer direction. During this time, you'll also want to offer support or help where necessary. Doing this step can help build your image and cause your network to have a positive image of who you are.

Boundaries and Preferences

Boundaries and preferences play a major role in our ability to connect. Respecting boundaries means:

- We understand that those we work with have limitations, agendas, and commitments of their own.
- Asking for permission before making any recommendations, introductions, or referrals. This means asking before sharing personal information.
- Respecting things such as time, privacy, and communication preferences such as limits on when you can contact them. Always ensure that your responses or follow-ups are done promptly.
- Minding how we behave and ensuring that we are not pushy, intrusive, or forward.

These are simple rules that can ensure smooth communication between all your connections in your network.

Networking is about sharing our resources. When we are open to sharing, we're opening ourselves up to also being of help to others. By being generous and helpful, we can show that we aren't just in the connection to gain something, but we're also willing to give.

Mentorship and Support Systems

A mentor is someone who teaches and offers assistance and advice to those who are less experienced within a certain field. The mentor uses their skills, knowledge, expertise, and resources to assist the person they are mentoring.

Mentorship refers to the relationship that a mentor has with their mentee, which is based on offering the mentee all the skills and resources needed for them to make it in a certain field. Keep in mind that mentorship isn't always formal, we can find ourselves having an informal mentor. In this section, we dissect mentorship and support systems.

The Role of Mentorship in Personal and Professional Relationships

Now that we understand what mentorship means, we can take a look at the role it plays in our personal and professional relationships.

Shared Knowledge and Skills

Joining a mentorship program or seeking a mentor means that you want to grow on a professional and personal level. Mentors can transfer or share their knowledge and expertise, which can help to broaden our horizons and help us make better decisions. Overall, mentorship offers us a competitive edge based on knowledge, experience, expertise, insights, and best practices.

Career Guidance and Support

Embarking on any journey requires that we have the necessary support. Mentors can offer us personalized guidance and support. Everything within the mentorship program is tailored to fit your needs and lifestyle.

Building Confidence

Knowing we're in safe hands and that we have the necessary support and guidance to build our careers can help us build confidence. This accompanied by our mentor's confidence in their skills and ability to lead can give us the confidence boost we need.

Networking and Creating Professional Connections

Having experience in a field usually means that you have the necessary connections to push another forward. This is one of the many benefits that comes with having a mentor, as their connections could change the trajectory of your career.

Encourage Diversity and Inclusion

One of the many issues we may face with achieving our dreams is the lack of inclusivity a certain field may have. Mentors can combat this issue by representing and collaborating with people from different backgrounds. This offers underrepresented groups a foot in the door and the chance to showcase what value they can bring to the table.

Knowledge Preservation

When we hand something of value down from one person to another, we can ensure continuity. Mentors assist in preserving knowledge by passing information, practices, and more down from one person to the next. Not only does this offer you a competitive edge, but it also offers you the chance to be exposed to what truly happens in certain fields.

Career Advancement

Investing in a mentor can lead to long-term career advancement and job satisfaction. A mentor is meant to assist you to grow and from this growth; we can feel more satisfied and confident in the positions we hold.

Mentors can play a major role in the success of their mentees, but how do we find a good mentor and what is our relationship supposed to look like?

How to Find a Mentor and Build a Productive Mentor-Mentee Relationship

Finding a good mentor can prove to be tricky, especially when it's your first time. You may find yourself struggling with a variety of things, including choosing the right one for you, how you can reach out to them, and how you can maintain that relationship. In this section, we answer all your questions while offering you practical tools to get you on your way.

Find the Mentor

For many of us, one of the many questions we ask ourselves is centered around how we can find the right mentor for us. Start by running through a list of people who have positively contributed and impacted your work. From there, make a list of who specializes in your field and has added value to your skills.

Request Your First Meeting

To start the process of mentorship we need to get into contact with the few mentors we may have shortlisted. Although this may be uncomfortable, we must understand that it is necessary and imperative for our growth. This means pushing through fear and any doubts we may have about the process.

When initiating contact, you'll want to avoid asking for mentorship; however, you can introduce yourself, state what you're busy with, and allude to your interest in their work and how it has positively impacted your life. From this point, you'll request a meeting, whether virtual or in-person. Make sure that the meeting is happening casually so you may want to ask that you have a virtual coffee with them. Keep the message as light, fluffy, and friendly as possible. During your interaction with them, you'll want to take note of chemistry and personality to find out if they are the right fit for you. Ensure that the meeting is brief but long enough for you to gather a feel of who they are.

Nurture the Relationship

Ensure that you get to know your mentor during your initial meeting. Ask them about their interests, hobbies, overall journey, and more. Keep it as casual and free as possible so that you are both yourselves during the meeting. Halfway through the meeting, it may be appropriate to bring up any questions you may have about your career and your wishes to grow. When wrapping up the call you might want to bring up some of their advice and your plans on using it. After the meeting, you can send in a thank you email or message just to thank them for their time and the many things you learned during your meeting together.

Conduct a Follow-Up

A few weeks after sending your message, you may want to follow up with your potential mentor. Consider this as a type of check-in to let them know what you did with their advice. In this email or message, you'll want to ask for another meeting; however, do not make this seem formal. With that being said, come up with a list of questions you'd like to ask.

Usually, after about three to four meetings later you'll have a good feel of who they are and whether or not this would be a good fit for you. You would have also established a type of relationship with them, making it easier for you to make your intentions known if you do decide to pursue them.

In the fourth or third meeting, you'll want to speak about your intentions to make them your mentor, as they have already contributed positively toward your life and overall career.

Maintain the Relationship/ Connection

Ever so often, you'll want to update your mentor on the progress happening in your life. At this point, meetings will become a regular occurrence, so you'll want to keep them in the loop about what you're doing and how they're helping you. You can also throw in a few questions you may want to ask about your current project or career goal.

Keep in mind that all relationships are meant to be reciprocal, meaning that both parties are meant to contribute. Offer to help with anything you can to let them know that this is not simply about work but a deeper connection. After every meeting, thank them for their time and efforts. Every thank you note doesn't have to be as extensive as your first, but you can still send it in.

Being a Mentor: Roles and Responsibilities

Now that we have a solid understanding of what a mentee can do, it's time to focus on the mentor. To effectively be a mentor, we need to understand our roles and responsibilities. In this section, we take a look at the different roles and responsibilities a mentor can have.

Provide Encouragement and Motivation

A mentor is meant to provide you with encouragement and motivation throughout your journey with them. This could be from both a personal and professional level.

Act as Role Models

One of the many roles a mentor will play in your life is the role of a role model due to their experience. This is because they are a prime example of professionalism, positive values, and integrity. Their main role is to showcase the behavior they'd like to see from their clients.

Offer Feedback

To grow we need to know what we're doing and what works. Our mentors are meant to look into our processes and systems and let us know where there is room for improvement. This feedback can help us achieve career goals and improve our personal lives.

Career Guidance

A mentor is meant to provide us with invaluable career guidance to help us along the journey of improvement. Due to them being experts in our fields, we can successfully navigate through the hurdles that come with our career and personal choices.

Helps Us to Set Goals

For us to grow, we need to set goals and keep track of how we're doing in those goals. As a mentor, their job is to assist us set goals that we can attain and help us come up with a plan to attain them. This offers our mentoring direction while targeting vital parts of our lives and careers.

Growth Acceleration

The main goal of a mentor is to help the mentee grow and accelerate their career and personal life. To do this, the mentor will try to develop personal and professional skills as well as offer feedback dedication and guidance. Simultaneously, the mentor will also push for more productivity and organization which ultimately helps to accelerate growth.

Offer Connections and Help Identify Resources

Our ability to network plays a major role in our ability to accelerate our careers. A mentor is supposed to offer as many resources as possible to help with success, one of those resources being connections. The more we're able to network with the right people, the more we'll find ourselves in better situations with our careers.

Connections can come in different forms, which include e-books, courses, technology to make processes easier, and more. Either way, connections and resources are meant to assist with learning, growth, and development.

Active Listening

A mentor's ability to listen is vital, especially because they are meant to people. To do this, people need to be comfortable enough to share their concerns, issues, questions, and perspectives without the fear of judgment or criticism.

Mentors play a major role in our ability to succeed, especially when they handle their roles and responsibilities well. If you feel as though your mentor is not offering what you're looking for, it's always best to seek out another mentor who can offer you the assistance you need.

Peer Support and Collaboration for Mutual Growth

In recent years, the professional space has changed drastically, with more professionals seeking better and more modern ways of gaining information and advancing their careers. Not only are professionals taking up short courses, but they are changing the way we view mentorship as a whole with the introduction and use of peer-to-peer coaching.

Peer-to-peer coaching focuses on mutual learning and growth among equals. The idea is for mentors and mentees to share experience and industry-specific information, which encourages collaboration between individuals. This form of mentoring allows for different perspectives to be shared while simultaneously offering networking opportunities to those who may not have previously had access to them.

Additionally, professionals are exposed to multiple mentors at once instead of relying on one mentor. This helps to broaden the thinking of professionals while also exposing them to different ways of thinking and problem-solving. The connections we form while participating in peer-to-peer coaching afford us the chance to collaborate, gain a broader understanding of our industry, and lead us to new opportunities.

Advantages of Peer-to-peer Coaching

There are four main advantages of peer-to-peer coaching which include:

- a shared empathy and understanding
- enhanced learning opportunities
- accountability and motivation
- diversity and networking opportunities

Peer-to-peer coaching is meant to expand our thinking while also assisting us to be accountable and motivated.

The idea is to allow everyone to share their ideas, knowledge, and expertise to help make the mentorship journey beneficial to everyone and create a space where both mentor and mentee are understood.

SPECIAL RELATIONSHIPS AND SITUATIONS

Romantic Relationships

As people, we have an innate longing for love and belonging, although we may find these in certain social relationships, romantic relationships offer us a deeper sense of connection, belonging, and understanding. A romantic relationship can be described and defined as a mutual and voluntary connection between two people that is ongoing. What makes a romantic relationship stand out is the physical and emotional intimacy that may be shared with those in the relationship. In this section, we take a deeper look into romantic relationships and the different things we can do to build and maintain them.

Building and Maintaining Healthy Romantic Relationships

A healthy relationship allows for trust, honesty, open communication, effort, and compromise from both parties. This means that there is no imbalance of power and both parties contribute positively toward the relationship. Additionally, there is mutual respect for one's independence ensuring that both parties can share their ideas, needs, and wants without fear that there will be retaliation.

A common misconception centered around healthy relationships is that they are based on the 50/50 rule. Originally, the 50/50 rule was created to ensure that there is equality in the relationship; however, it has evolved to the sharing of duties, finances, and overall decision-making. Some may argue that the 50/50 rule pushes parties to keep a record of whether or not their partner is contributing while others argue that a healthy relationship is about recognizing the needs of your partner and filling in the gap.

Either way, healthy relationship dynamics are centered around what works for the couple rather than societal norms. By communicating your boundaries earlier on in the relationship and having conversations centered around relationship dynamics, you can find a middle ground that can help your relationship to remain healthy. Although this is true, there are a few general characteristics of a healthy relationship which include:

- respect for privacy and space
- ability to express opinions and concerns
- safety in all aspects including physical, emotional, financial, spiritual, and psychological
- general respect for your feelings and wishes with all conflict being resolved through compromise and negotiation
- freedom to spend time with family, friends, or even alone

Building and Maintaining a healthy relationship requires that we focus on the basics of a healthy relationship which include:

Boundaries

In a previous chapter, we discussed the importance of setting boundaries and how we can set them. In this section, we take another look at boundaries in the context of healthy romantic relationships.

One of the key foundations of a healthy relationship is having and setting boundaries. This outlines what we can and cannot do within the relationship. Usually, when healthy people come together, they have personal boundaries with a few being centered around relationships. When the two get together, they can discuss the boundaries of their relationship concerning their boundaries.

Realistically, we cannot speak to our partners about all the boundaries we may have; however, we can voice our opinions when we feel uncomfortable about doing certain things. Along the line, we may discover other boundaries which we can communicate with our partner. Keep in mind that our partners are human beings meaning that when we dislike or are uncomfortable about something we must voice our opinion. When boundaries are constantly being crossed or disrespected, it may be time to leave.

Communication

Our ability to communicate in our relationships is important as it affords us the chance to voice our opinions on matters that are dear to us. Being unable to effectively communicate can lead to issues such as misunderstanding and hurt feelings.

Effective communication is centered around our ability to voice our opinion while making sure that our statements do not attack the other party. Additionally, we are meant to use our active listening skills to ensure that we hear and understand the other party's reasoning and feelings toward the situation. While doing this we'll want to ensure that our body language or demeanor allows for the other party to feel comfortable with having the conversation.

When trying to communicate feelings or needs you'll want to do so in person. This limits or cancels out any room for misinterpretation. Always ensure that you have conversations in environments that are calm as this helps to maintain peace.

Trust

Building trust can take time especially when there have been issues with trust in the past. We may also experience issues with trust due to previous partners who broke our trust. When placed in this situation it's always best to isolate issues to ensure that you aren't blaming current partners for the mistakes and issues of previous partners.

Building trust can be tricky; however, there are ways for us to build trust. Firstly, we can start by being as reliable as possible. This means sticking to our word and showing up when we say we will.

Secondly, we'll need to focus on respecting the boundaries of our partners. This means taking stock of the boundaries they have placed and making sure that we abide by them.

Thirdly, we need to be as honest as possible. Building trust is about transparency which can only be achieved through honesty between two partners. The more honest we are, the easier it is for our partner to trust us and our opinions.

Trust is built when we are open, honest, and able to respect the boundaries of our partner. The point is to keep our word and show up for them when they need us. The more we do these things, the easier it is for our partner to trust us.

Consent

Consent in a romantic relationship isn't something that is openly discussed. This is because many of us assume that because we are in a romantic relationship with someone, we automatically have consent for all things which couldn't be further from the truth.

Building and maintaining healthy romantic relationships requires work. The more we express our differences the more we may find ourselves in situations of conflict. In the next section, we take a deeper look into conflict and communication.

Communication and Conflict Resolution in Romantic Relationships

Dealing with conflict in a romantic relationship is inevitable and can be brought up due to a difference in opinion. How we view and deal with conflict can have a major impact on our romantic relationships and the partners within them. When we see conflict as a problem rather than an opportunity to grow, we hinder ourselves from the experience of learning our partners. In this section, we take a deeper look into communication and conflict resolution.

Healthy Communication

Healthy communication happens when we can effectively express our ideas, thoughts, and emotions. This means that we afford everyone the chance to speak without us or them interjecting. Additionally, we are devoted to the exchange and are mindful of our behavior.

Keep in mind that healthy communication is required for long-term relationships to assist with overall intimacy and satisfaction. The manner we use to communicate has a direct impact on how we resolve conflict in romantic relationships. When we have healthy ways to communicate, we can resolve conflict in a healthy manner making the relationship more conducive for all.

Additionally, healthy communication can assist us in finding different ways to handle conflict. For example, we can adjust the tone of our communication according to the needs of the situation. Perhaps we need to be more stern or we need to be affectionate and provide validation. Either way, healthy communication can assist with many things in the relationship and can cause us to become more vulnerable, open, and honest.

How to Handle Conflict Using Healthy Communication

Engaging in conflict can be something we tend to shy away from especially when we have trauma that is associated with any form of conflict. Becoming dismissive, aggressive, disassociating, or avoidant can be a result of past trauma associated with conflict. Healthy communication can assist us in navigating conflict effectively while also creating an environment where our previous conflict-coping mechanisms do not have to arise. You can handle conflict using healthy communication by:

Isolate the Incident

Oftentimes, heated discussions are centered around past conflicts that we feel were not resolved to our satisfaction. Additionally, we may feel as though bringing up past conflict during a present disagreement can show patterns and general dissatisfaction with how the previous conflict was handled. This approach, although seemingly helpful, can bring about other major issues and cause conflict to be ongoing.

Isolating the incident and keeping all facts, thoughts, and emotions in the present argument can help majorly with effective conflict resolution. It affords us the chance to see the situation for what it is rather than passing on any aggression or previous issues that can make us lose focus on the current disagreement.

Listen With Intention

The manner we listen to others has a direct impact on whether or not we can understand their argument or defense. For this reason, we must take stock of how we listen during conflict. Are we listening to respond or defend or are we listening to understand?

Listening with intention, or active listening, can assist us in truly hearing the argument of the other party. This can help us during conflict resolution and make navigating arguments a lot easier.

See Things From Their Point of View

Have you ever been in a disagreement with someone and felt as though their opinion was the only one that mattered? Unfortunately, this may be the same experience we offer to others when we are in an argument. To combat this issue, we will need to put ourselves in the next person's shoes and see things from their perspective. This will require patience, active listening, and the asking of questions where we feel we don't understand.

Respond to Criticism With Empathy

Criticism is not something many of us enjoy hearing especially when it comes from our partners. We may feel as though they are unappreciative or simply taking jabs at our character. Although we may feel this way, this is not always the case.

Healthy criticism in a romantic relationship can assist us in becoming better people while also helping us cater to the needs of our partner. Instead of seeing their criticism as a personal attack, we can start seeing it as a way to improve thus lowering our guard and defense mechanisms allowing us to show empathy toward them.

Keep in mind that there is both healthy and unhealthy criticism. If you feel as though your partner is overly critical of you and your actions, you may want to seek additional advice from a professional or family member.

Take Personal Responsibility

Our ability to take responsibility for our actions can play a major role in our ability to resolve conflict. When take responsibility for the part we play in an argument, we show maturity and the ability to take responsibility which can help to defuse the situation.

Take Notice of Your Statements

During arguments, we may be tempted to disregard how we speak to our partners. Although this is done out of frustration, it can lead to multiple issues. When engaging in conflict, you'll want to try and use statements that are centered around your feelings and how certain things made you feel. This ensures that we are not attacking the next person but are simply making them understand how certain actions or statements made us feel.

Learn to Compromise

Changing our mentality from winning the argument to seeking a solution that works for everyone can help resolve conflict. This is because the solution is not coming at the expense of someone else's peace or boundaries. Compromising can ensure that both you and your partner are happy with the result of the argument.

Take a Break

One of the many things that can help with conflict resolution is taking a break during an argument. This method works well if you feel as though the argument is escalating and becoming unhealthy.

By taking a break you can afford yourself the opportunity to calm down and think of the issue or matter at hand. This affords us clarity and a better opportunity to look into the feelings of others. Do your best to continue to have the conversation until both parties feel that it has been resolved satisfactorily.

When all else fails, it's always a good idea to ask for assistance from a third party. Counseling or seeking therapy is not something to be ashamed of and can assist you with finding healthier and better solutions.

Dealing with conflict can be terrifying; however, when we are well-equipped we can afford ourselves the tools we need to combat the issue.

Balancing Romance With Personal Independence

Our ability to build and maintain a healthy relationship is based on our ability to maintain a balance between our relationship and our independence. Many would refer to this equilibrium as a type of yin and yang situation that requires absolute balance for both romantic partners to feel valued, seen, and heard.

Our independence refers to our need for individuality in our relationship. This means that we are afforded personal space, autonomy, and self-expression through our ability to continue to pursue our interests, hobbies, and goals.

To be independent within the relationship does not mean that we are detached or lack any form of commitment. Instead, it means that we can focus on personal growth, and maintaining our identity while also having the ability to respect the boundaries of our partner. Autonomy can also reduce the risk of us becoming codependent on our partners.

On the other hand, togetherness or oneness within the relationship is just as important. Oneness affords us the chance to build stronger binds allowing for intimacy and a deeper emotional connection. Keep in mind that oneness plays a major role in how well or poorly we're able to make decisions together, and our ability to tackle challenges while also affecting how well we can achieve common goals.

Oneness also affords us the chance to offer emotional support and create memories. Finding balance or creating space for balance will require a lot of work especially when you are working toward creating a healthy environment. Equilibrium between togetherness and independence may take a while to find and will require that we set boundaries, communicate openly, ensure we schedule for quality time, and pursue our interests while also maintaining flexibility.

Various rewards come with maintaining balance which include:

- achieving a harmonious relationship where everyone feels loved, supported, and respected
- growth within our personal spaces and goals
- achieved longevity as there is room to grow in both personal and relationship spaces
- a greater sense of happiness and satisfaction
- reduction in conflict

Finding a balance between oneness and independence is vital especially when we're headed toward the common goal of freedom and comfort.

Navigating the Challenges of Long-Term Relationships

Managing and maintaining long-term relationships can prove to be difficult especially when one is changing and the other isn't. We can find ourselves losing touch with one another creating emotional and physical gaps in the relationship. Additionally, we may find ourselves losing the deep emotional connection we once had causing us to turn into roommates rather than partners.

Navigating these issues can quickly turn into an extreme sport especially when we have no idea what we're doing. In this section, we offer you a few tips and tricks to help you navigate the challenges of long-term relationships.

Start With Communication

When you think of a healthy long-term relationship what comes to mind? Do you think of their ability to make things work or do you think of their ability to communicate well? All relationships require that we are present and willing to work on them. One of the many things that come with trying to navigate the challenges of a long-term relationship is communication.

Throughout this book, we have mentioned and spoken about communication many times. This is because communication is the lifeblood of all relationships whether personal or professional. Our proficiency in communication can either hinder or progress our relationships.

Navigating through the issues that come with being in a long-term relationship is heavily based on our ability to communicate how we feel about certain issues. Long-term relationships require that we are in constant communication to avoid instances where there are gaps in communication resulting in misunderstandings. By keeping or maintaining open communication we can work through any issues that may arise including those that come with being in a long-term relationship.

Quality Time

One of the many issues long-term relationships face is issues concerning connection and intimacy. Quality time occurs when we spend time with our partner without any distractions. This means putting away social media, laptops, and any other device or thing that may cause a distraction. We are present in the moment with our partner, catering to our relationship and our needs.

Making It Through Tough Times

Life will always present us with ups and downs that affect those we love or are in a relationship with. The key to whether our relationship succeeds or fails lies in our ability to make it through those tough times. Unresolved issues can lead to issues with trust, anger, or resentment which can contribute toward the downfall of your relationship.

Navigating conflict or other issues in any relationship is hard. When things feel as though they are becoming out of control or a resolution is nowhere in sight, it is always best to seek help from a third party. Try choosing an individual who has knowledge of both your personalities and can remain as objective as possible. If this doesn't work, look for help from a therapist. There may be a few underlying issues at play that can only be brought to the surface through counseling and therapy.

Family Dynamics

One of the trickiest relationships to work through is the one we have with our families. In this section, we take a look at family dynamics and the different things you can do to try and work through or improve your family dynamics and the relationships associated with them.

Understanding and Appreciating Family Roles and Relationships

To understand family roles and relationships, we first need to understand what a family is. A family can be described as two or more individuals who are related through birth, adoption, or marriage. Family bonds can also be formed in situations where individuals share an emotional bond or tie that resembles that of a family member. For example, an aunt or grandmother may play the role of a mother to a child. This child may see their aunt or grandmother as a mother figure and may even resort to calling them their mother. Similar situations may also occur for an uncle or grandfather. Either way, the role of a family member is being assumed by an individual who otherwise would not have played that role under normal circumstances.

Our immediate family consists of our parents, children, spouse, or siblings while our extended family includes grandparents, aunts, uncles, cousins, nephews, in-laws, and more. Families come in different sizes and may include nuclear, joint, or blended families. A nuclear family consists of a couple and their children while a joint family is made up of a couple, their children, and grandchildren. Blended families, on the other hand, consist of a couple, their children from previous relationships or marriages, and any children that they may have had together.

Family bonds and ties are important as they provide us with a sense of stability, and well-being and play a significant role in our mental growth. Family bonds and their experiences can help to shape children and their ability to form healthy or unhealthy bonds later on in life. Family bonds also assist us to:

- have a safe space where we know we are accepted despite our shortcomings
- provide us with a sense of comfort knowing that there will always be people by our side in good and bad times
- teach us how to build trust and be there in both good and bad times for those we love
- play a fundamental part in the way we see conflict and our ability to resolve it as adults

Keep in mind that all families and their dynamics are different resulting in many of us having different experiences of what family is meant to be. Although this is true, there are a few commonalities that can be found in strong and healthy families which include:

- good communication
- togetherness
- quality time
- are and affection shown to every member of the family
- support
- seeing conflict or crisis as an opportunity to grow
- a shared concern for everyone's well-being
- and resilience.

Keep in mind that growth and stability require that every member of the family contribute toward growth and overall wellness. Building a strong family may not come naturally to all; however, building one is possible. We can build a strong family by:

- spending quality time together as a family
- maintaining and ensuring that there is good communication among everyone in the family
- honoring and showing appreciation toward everyone in the family

- celebrating autonomy and individuality through appreciating and accepting talents, strengths, and differences
- working on current issues as a team
- establishing clear and healthy boundaries and rules
- teaching children about conflict resolution and forgiveness. For parents, this means leading by example especially when conflict arises

One of the major issues experienced in families is their inability to resolve conflict in a manner that is healthy and works well for everyone. Building a strong family isn't about what people see on the outside but how healthy and functional the relationships are when they aren't exposed to the public. We can work on building Strong family dynamics by working on ourselves and recognizing and accepting our shortcomings. A good place to go or start would be to attend counseling or seek a therapist who can help us deal with any internal issues.

Effective Communication Within Family Units

Family units can benefit tremendously from effective communication that is open, honest, and respectful. How we communicate can have a tremendous effect on our family dynamics and whether or not we can keep them healthy. When we can communicate effectively, we're able to communicate our ideas without fear of judgment which can contribute toward how a conversation turns out.

When we have good communication skills we're able to effectively express our feelings, thoughts, and emotions between our family members. Communication is something we can learn and benefit from especially in family dynamics. This is because when we improve our communication we can better express ourselves leading to fewer misunderstandings or arguments which can enrich our relationships.

When we're unable to communicate effectively in family dynamics we may find ourselves in constant conflict that goes unresolved. This can lead to a strain in the relationship while also causing issues with trust. Issues in communication can massively affect parent-child relationships especially if either party feels as though they are not being heard.

Many times, we can attribute poor communication to barriers that exist within family circles. These barriers can include:

- inability to convey feelings in a manner that can be heard
- issues with active listening and empathy
- jumping to conclusions
- constant interjections
- and using past trauma to view a situation

To overcome these barriers we need to implement effective communication strategies. These will ensure that we minimize the chances of being misunderstood and having issues with further conflict.

Strategies for Effective Communication

One of the best strategies to combat issues with communication is active listening. In previous chapters, we have focused immensely on active listening and its impact on overall communication. Within family dynamics, active listening can help us combat issues that are associated with misunderstandings such as feeling as though your points are not valid.

To implement active listening we can ask follow-up questions while also doing our best to avoid giving solutions immediately. The point is to ask a question and hear what they have to say first before making assumptions or giving a solution.

One of the many mistakes we make during arguments is proving our point. To effectively communicate, we need to afford everyone the chance to speak and voice their opinion. This is most important during conflict resolution to try to improve family dynamics.

Handling Family Conflicts and Resolving Issues

All families face some form of conflict because although they are a family, they still have different beliefs, values, and perspectives that may clash. Keep in mind that occasional conflict is normal; however, we may find ourselves experiencing constant conflict resulting in ill feelings toward family members. When this happens conflict then becomes unhealthy and can pose a threat to a family bond.

Common causes of conflict vary from family to family; nevertheless, there are a few common causes of conflict that have been found which include:

- moving in together as a couple
- the birth of a child or other children
- a teenager transitioning into adulthood
- and or a child becoming a teenager

Different stages of life can cause conflict especially when the parties involved would like to do things differently. Other major topics of conflict can be attributed to major changes in family circumstances such as:

- divorce
- changes in finances
- moving homes or a country
- long-distance traveling for work and more

When change takes place, especially within family dynamics it usually results in conflict because different family members will need different things. At times, the change is unavoidable making some or one family member feel as though their feelings are not considered. Navigating such issues can be difficult which is why we've offered a few strategies to help alleviate the pressures of handling conflict.

Agree to Negotiate

Conflict arises when we refuse to listen to the argument of another which makes finding a peaceful resolution almost utterly impossible. Negotiating and listening to different views can be an effective way of handling conflict. During the process of negotiation, you'll want to take into account:

- whether or not the issue holds any form of importance
- separating the conflict at hand from the person
- taking breaks to help when emotions are high
- letting go of the idea that the next person has to agree with you
- showing that you respect the other person's perspective by listening and paying attention
- finding places for common ground
- and agreeing to disagree

Listen

Arguments escalate when we're set on not compromising or even hearing the next person's argument. When this happens, it causes a misunderstanding and can escalate the disagreement. When this happens, try your best to remain as calm as possible while doing your best to put your feelings aside. Try your best to listen to understand the points and views and ensure that you don't interrupt them as they speak. After hearing their argument, ask questions to clarify anything you are confused about and then communicate your side of the story. During this time, do your best to avoid bringing up old disagreements that went unresolved.

Work Together

Solutions can only be found when we work together as a team. Working jointly for the betterment of the family can help to find a solution and implement that solution. Try your best to ensure that everyone has been considered during this time.

When you feel as though no resolution can be found, it may be a good idea to ask or seek professional help.

Adapting to Changes in Family Dynamics

Changes in family dynamics can be uncomfortable especially when a dramatic change to the family situation is also looming. This can bring about feelings of anxiety, discomfort, and overall issues in our ability to see things as one as a family. For this reason, adapting to change is imperative especially when wanting to maintain healthy family relationships.

Get to Know Each Other Again

Getting to know your family member again may seem a little out of pocket considering that they are your family. Although this is true, changes in family dynamics can drastically change who people are and the role they play in our lives. By getting to know them again, we let go of the pressures of who they were and embrace the new version of them and while also embracing the new role they may have assumed. During this time, you'll want to be intentional about spending time with them meaning that you can eat together, play games together, go on a walk or hike, or even take a trip together where possible. The point is to engage in conversation in an easy-going environment that allows for conversation and the creation of shared memories and experiences.

Invest in the Relationship

Oftentimes, changes in dynamics can leave us disappointed and resistant to trying again. This means that we may shy away from investing in the relationship. Even though this may be true and our concerns may be valid, investing in a relationship is one of the best ways to help us adapt to changes in the family.

When we're invested, we're willing to try again and put in the work required to make the situation work despite the change. This means that we are present, aware of the change, and willing to work around it.

Keep in mind that change in family dynamics leaves room for change in family traditions. This is something new and exciting that all family members can participate in making it a bonding experience. Family traditions and rituals can also work to honor those we may have lost or gained along the way.

Friendships Across Life Stages

Friendship is the win of life. –Edward Young

One of the best social relationships we can have, outside of family, is friendships. Friendships can have a profound effect on our mental and emotional health and can assist us in avoiding things such as loneliness and isolation. When healthy, friendships can contribute toward a healthy purposeful, and fulfilling life.

The Evolution of Friendships From Adulthood to Childhood

The more we journey through life, the more apparent change becomes not only with our appearance but within the way we manage ourselves and the friendships we hold dear. For many of us, childhood friends are one of our most cherished friendships as they played a vital part in our years of development. Although this is true, we may find ourselves at a crossing especially when we begin our journey to adulthood. Any adult can attest to how busy life becomes the older we get. Many of us experience the pressures of being an adult such as finances, losses, and the simple pressure of having to get our life together. This makes trying to maintain friendships difficult with many childhood friends complaining of the gap that adulthood brings especially in friendships that were formed during childhood. We can combat this gap through:

Quality Over Quantity

Being intentional about our time as adults is vital especially when trying to maintain a friendship. Setting aside time for catch-up sessions, meet-ups, trips and more can assist in maintaining the bond between yourself and your friends. Not only does this help maintain friendships but it can also assist us in understanding the life dynamics of our friends. Having this knowledge gives us the tools we need to work through our friendships effectively because we know when and how we can add value to our friendships.

Celebrate Milestones

Friendships are centered around support and celebration. When friendship evolves from childhood to adulthood the nature of what we celebrate changes, with this being said, all milestones whether great or small should be celebrated. When we offer celebration we show that our friendships are not purely based on honoring the friendship we had in the past but are active ongoing friendships that we continue to nurture. Outside of celebrating milestones, we need to continue to ensure that our friends know and understand that we support them and see their value.

Embrace Growth

Issues in friendships occur when we refuse to accept that growth may change us or those around us. The idea is that everything is meant to remain the same and when the opposite happens, we may find ourselves struggling to maintain or engage with friends.

Embracing growth can be an amazing way to combat issues that come with growth. Embracing change means accepting our friends for who they are and the changes that come with their personal growth. Once this has been achieved, we're able to move past any jealousy or negative emotions that may come with their growth. This could mean accepting and adjusting to a new job in a different country, marriages, children being birthed, and more. The point is to work around change to help build the relationship.

Maintaining Long Distance Friendships

There is magic in long-distance friendships. They let you relate to other human beings in a way that goes beyond being physically together and is often more profound. –Diana Cortes

The reality of life is that it scatters us across the globe the more we seek greener pastures. This means leaving behind our hometowns and forfeiting the benefit of having childhood friends nearby. Thanks to technological advancements, our friends may be far in distance, but they need not be far in communication or heart. We can keep our friends and family in the loop of what's going on through social media platforms making it easier to connect and communicate. Although this is true, there are other ways to help maintain your long-distance friendship.

Be Intentional

To maintain a long-distance friendship, we need to be intentional about our efforts toward it. While doing this, we also need to speak to our friends about our intentions of maintaining the friendship and the different plans we will put in place to achieve this. This is because friendship is a two-way street meaning that our friends will also need to participate in maintaining the friendship.

Utilize Common Interests

Take a moment to think about your friendships from the perspective of common interests. What do you find as the anchor to your friendships? An anchor is a common interest that both of you may have that triggers one to contact the other. This can be anything at all including cooking, reading a book, or watching a movie or series, for as long as it is something you both enjoy. Of course, friendships are not only maintained through an anchor, but it can be an amazing trigger to get you in contact.

Vulnerability can also be an amazing tool to help maintain the friendship. The more there's distance between us, the harder we may find it to be vulnerable with our friends. When we are vulnerable, we invite our friends to be vulnerable with us making it easier for us to maintain our connection.

Reach Out

One of the greatest fears we may have in a friendship is rejection. By reaching out to our friends when there are issues, we afford them the opportunity of knowing that we value their friendship and are willing to talk about issues to save the friendship.

When we feel like the issue is beyond something we can fix over a phone call schedule a visitation. Physical contact is one of the best tools to help mend a friendship and can remind you of why you are in the friendship in the first place.

Resolve Conflict

Being in a long-distance friendship is tricky and may open doors for us to leave issues unresolved. Although this may seem like a reasonable thing to do it can leave your friendship in shambles.

In previous chapters, we touched on conflict and the different conflict resolution tactics you can use to assist you. Try using these conflict resolution tactics and find the best way that works for you and your friend. Remember, conflict is an opportunity for us to learn and should be used and treated as such.

Finding the best way to maintain your friendship can be slightly exhausting. Not only are you working on your own life and the adjustments that come with moving but you're also trying to hold your friendships together. During this time, you may find that certain friendships may fall apart. In the next section, we tackle how you can effectively revive your friendships and when it's time to simply let go.

Reviving Old Friendships and When to Let Go

Friendships, just like normal relationships, go through ups and downs with quite a few not being able to survive on their own. Although this is true, reconnecting with old friends is possible especially when both parties are willing to work on the relationship.

Keep in mind that reconnecting doesn't mean that we simply press play on the relationship and things go back to normal. It means that we are willing to work on the relationship and do our best to reconnect because things didn't work out the previous time. There are various ways to reconnect which include:

Start By Thinking

Before making any decisions about reaching rekindling your friendship you'll want to take the time to ponder on what truly happened and the reasons why you may have let go of the friendship. Was their inability to listen to a problem or was there a major betrayal that led to the two of you ending things?

Toxic behavior or abuse are always good reasons to end a friendship. If the friendship became mentally or emotionally draining, then it would be a good time to end the friendship. Usually, when going back to old relationships we go in the hopes that the next person would have changed but this is not always the case. If they are exhibiting similar behavior or do not show any remorse for their actions, you may want to continue on the path of letting them go.

Start on a Clean Slate

Once the decision to pursue the friendship has been reached, you'll want to try and start on a clean slate. Starting on a clean slate means that you afford everyone the privilege of settling into friendship and learning new habits and boundaries. In other words, start as acquaintances to get well acquainted with each other again.

Keep in mind that the need for reconciliation may not be for everyone. So, it's always best to extend your hand while also leaving room for disappointment.

Afford Them Time to Process Everything

In our haste to acquire our friendship, let us not push too hard that it pushes the next person away. Rekindling a friendship is tricky as other parties may not be so keen to rekindle. By affording them the chance to break down what happened and process the events and their feelings you make room for them to make a final decision on whether or not they think your friendship may work. Remember that outside of your friendship, they are people too and have other things that may need to take priority.

Maintaining friendships and relationships as an adult is hard work and will require that you are fully engaged in making things work. Part of the process is knowing when to let go of a friendship you may feel is killing your ability to function normally. If you are experiencing abuse or feel as though you are emotionally or mentally drained, it may be time to call it quits. Friendships are a two-way street, and we need to be giving as much as we are receiving.

Making New Friends in Different Stages of Life

As we transition in life, meet new people, and change we may want to acquire new friendships with people that can understand our lifestyle and the overall dynamics of our lives. Throughout life, we may find ourselves in need of friends or making new friends. Although our ways of making friends may differ there are a few rules that can assist us during this journey.

When trying to make new friends it's always best to remain as open-minded as possible because we never really know where our friendships may come from. This means talking to and engaging with people while not being focused on their appearance or on any preconceived ideas we may have of them.

Connecting with people means that we need to engage with them. For many of us, engaging and connecting with people may not be something we're used to. When connecting you'll want to remain as authentic so you can avoid attracting or engaging with people you are not able to maintain a connection with. If you're struggling to make a connection with someone try engaging in an activity that you can both bond over. Ask about their interests and work from there.

If you're truly struggling to take that first step, then perhaps look into utilizing social opportunities to try and make new friends.

When we're out and about we're in constant contact with people. By stopping and engaging with people we may find ourselves making new friends.

To create space for something new, we may need to let go of something old. At times, the friendships we keep around aren't necessarily serving us or growing us and may make us think that we have friends when truly we don't. By evaluating our current friendships, we can gauge the friends we truly have as opposed to believing that certain individuals are our friends when they serve no purpose.

Keep in mind that building social relationships is something that takes time and resilience. The more we become accustomed to engagement the less it will make us feel uncomfortable. You are capable of making new friends and keeping friendships and relationships perhaps you just haven't met your crowd of people.

CONCLUSION

Lifelong Journey of Relationship Building

Social relationships are something we will continuously need therefore making building relationships a lifelong journey.

Embracing the Continuous Learning Process in Relationships

The journey of life is a continuous learning curve. As we transition, we may change our circle of friends or those we are in a relationship with because of the needs that may arise with our lifestyle choices.

Embracing the learning process allows us to reach our personal and professional goals while also assisting us to learn new things about ourselves, the reality of life, and those around us.

We can embrace the learning process by allowing ourselves to learn together. When we learn together, we shift the power dynamic which can help to reset the friendship or relationship. We are also able to create shared memories and experiences.

We can also embrace the learning process through:

- spending more time together
- cultivating a spirit of curiosity within our friendships or relationships
- sharing our goals
- and having a beginner mindset

As we learn we grow and find better and healthier ways to adapt to different situations of life. By embracing change and the lifelong learning process we put ourselves in a better position to grow and nurture our relationships.

Adapting to Changes in Personal and Others' Lives

Change is constant and is something that we will constantly experience whether in our lives or the lives of those around us. As people, we adapt to change differently; however, there are a few universal rules that can assist us which include:

Remaining Positive

Our perspective of change can have a direct influence on how we behave during change in our own lives and those around us. When we're in a constant state of panic or fear, we see change negatively which can affect how we behave and advise others in their season of change. By having a positive mindset, we can shine the light of hope for ourselves and others.

Remember Your Goals

Amid change, we need to remember who we are and what we're capable of doing. When we remember these, we're able to move forward healthily. By keeping our goals in remembrance, we're able to navigate through the challenge of change in our lives and the lives of others.

Plan for Change

Most times, we are unprepared for Change which could be the reason why we experience it with so much frustration. Although all situations in life cannot be planned for, we can make an effort to plan for what we know may change. For example, we can change how we engage in conflict as many times this is inevitable.

How we behave and think has a direct impact on how we operate in the lives of others. When we are self-aware, we're able to manage ourselves and our emotions better.

The Importance of Self-Reflection and Growth in Relationship Skills

Self-reflection is a powerful tool that can be used for personal development and growth within relationships. When we engage in the journey of self-reflection, we prompt ourselves to look within and explore our thoughts, experiences, and emotions. The journey of self-reflection is filled with deep introspection, internal examination, and a willingness to explore ourselves and the reason we have become the way we are.

Embarking on the journey of self-reflection can make a positive contribution toward our relationship skills as we gain a clearer understanding of the role we play in relationships and the different ways our thoughts, emotions and overall behavior can impact others.

Self-reflection can also assist us in understanding our communication skills and the different ways we interpret the communication and words of others. Additionally, this process can help us understand our emotional habits and the emotional spaces we seem to be safe.

Future of Social Relationships

In the last 50 years, we have seen a drastic change in the way we interact. With technological advancements, we may be looking into future changes in social relationships.

Anticipating and Adapting to Future Trends in Social Interaction

Changes in social interaction have a direct impact on our social relationships and overall mental and emotional well-being. Social interactions assist us in building and maintaining social relationships, and how we express ourselves, and have a direct impact on our social skills. With technological advancements on the rise, we may find ourselves experiencing more things such as social isolation, a decrease in social skills, and an increase in anxiety and depression. To combat these issues and stay above changes we can:

- Increase our time with family and friends by attending family gatherings or planning and showing up to social events.
- Using technological advancements to nurture friendships and relationships.
- Striking a balance between social media and technological advancements with real-life human interaction.
- Being in the outdoors.
- Limiting time spent on social media or other technological advancements.

In previous chapters, we covered the effects of technology on social interaction. Staying above technological advancements can help to improve how we interact while also ensuring that we do not lose our social interaction skills.

Embracing Technology While Maintaining Authentic Connections

When using technology it's important to remember that it is simply a tool used to enhance our relationships and make connecting and communicating with each other easier. With that being said, technology is only to do as we instruct it meaning that how we use it is within our power and control.

Embracing technology does not mean that we need to abandon all ways of connecting. It simply means that we can enhance our experience. By striking a balance between technology and social interaction, we can ensure that our connections remain as authentic as possible.

The Ongoing Importance of Personal Relationships in an Evolving World

Personal relationships play a vital role in mental and emotional well-being and contribute toward living a healthy and happy life.

Researchers have uncovered that when we are a part of healthy relationships we can live longer, deal with stressful situations better, live healthier lives, and feel richer.

Social relationships and our ability to build them will continue to play a major role in society. For society to function and continue to remain connected we need to ensure that we learn how we can build, restore, and maintain the social relationships that keep us together.

As we venture into relationships with others, we learn about ourselves and the standards that we use to judge ourselves and others. Through the journey of self-exploration, we can build empathy and connect more easily with those around us.

THANKS FOR READING

Dear reader,

Thank you for reading *Building Good Social Relationships*.

If you enjoyed this book, please leave a review where you bought it. It helps more than most people think.

Don't forget your FREE book!

You will also be among the first to know of FREE review copies, discount offers, bonus content, and more.

Go to:

https://www.SFNonfictionBooks.com/Free-Book

Thanks again for your support.

AUTHOR RECOMMENDATIONS

Unlocking the Secrets to Purposeful Living

Embrace your potential, because a fulfilling life is waiting.

Get it now.

www.SFNonfictionBooks.com/Everyday-Ikigai

Unlock the Secrets of Your Mind

Nurture your mental well-being, because better brain health begins with knowledge.

Get it now.

www.SFNonfictionBooks.com/Map-Human-Brain

ABOUT SAM FURY

www.SamFury.com

Sam Fury has had a passion for survival, evasion, resistance, and escape (SERE) training since he was a young boy growing up in Australia.

This led him to years of training and career experience in related subjects, including martial arts, military training, and outdoor pursuits.

These days, he spends his time refining his skills and sharing what he learns via his books and blog.

amazon.com/stores/Sam-Fury/author/B00C8Z4U8S

facebook.com/SamFuryOfficial

instagram.com/samfuryofficial

youtube.com/@SamFuryOfficial

x.com/Samfuryoriginal

tiktok.com/@samfuryofficial

REFERENCES

https://braidedway.org/the-animate-everything/

https://doi.org/10.1007/978-1-4419-1005-9_59

https://doi.org/10.3758/s13428-022-01821-8

https://shakatribeshop.com/blogs/shaka-tribe-culture/balancing-independence-and-interdependence-in-relationships

www.addictions.com/blog/is-the-digital-age-to-blame-for-online-shopping-addiction/

www.baileythurley.com/community/necessity-making-new-friends-any-stage-life/

www.betterhealth.vic.gov.au/health/healthyliving/family-conflict

www.betterhealth.vic.gov.au/health/HealthyLiving/Strong-relationships-strong-health

www.betterhealth.vic.gov.au/health/HealthyLiving/Strong-relationships-strong-health#relationships-help-society-too

www.betterup.com/blog/how-to-build-rapport

www.betterup.com/blog/self-discovery-techniques

www.bidenschool.udel.edu/ipa/serving-delaware/crp/difficult-conversations

www.calmer-you.com/how-to-get-over-fear-of-rejection/

www.cdc.gov/emotional-wellbeing/social-connectedness/affect-health.htm#:~:text=Research%20shows%20that%20social%20connectedness

www.centerstone.org/our-resources/health-wellness/the-power-of-diverse-friendships/

www.coping.us/toolsforrelationships/handlingrelationshipbarriers.html

www.drexel.edu/graduatecollege/professional-development/blog/2018/july/five-types-of-communication/

www.elearningindustry.com/major-benefits-of-peer-to-peer-coaching

www.en.wikipedia.org/wiki/Social_relation

www.forbes.com/sites/forbescommunicationscouncil/2023/08/21/how-to-build-a-network-and-establish-meaningful-business-connections/?sh=6664b18a4456

www.forbes.com/sites/forbestechcouncil/2019/09/18/tech-and-its-impact-on-behavior/?sh=27b4aa8fb64b

www.gq.co.za/sex-relationships/6-signs-that-your-relationship-is-no-longer-working-and-does-not-make-you-happy-according-to-psychology-92be4477-35d9-490d-bb5a-80e1cc4b0fbb

www.graygroupintl.com/blog/self-reflection

www.hbr.org/2021/03/whats-the-right-way-to-find-a-mentor

www.healthdirect.gov.au/building-and-maintaining-healthy-relationships#:~:text=People%20who%20have%20healthy%20relationships

www.helpguide.org/articles/grief/dealing-with-a-breakup-or-divorce.htm

www.helpguide.org/articles/relationships-communication/setting-healthy-boundaries-in-relationships.htm

www.hongkiat.com/blog/online-vs-offline-social-life/

www.iidmglobal.com/expert_talk/expert-talk-categories/managing-people/staff_communication/id19068.html

www.indeed.com/career-advice/career-development/handling-difficult-conversations

www.jillianturecki.com/blog/how-do-you-know-when-to-end-a-toxic-relationship

www.kaspersky.com/resource-center/definitions/what-is-a-digital-footprint

www.libguides.trschools.k12.wi.us/evaluatingnews/netiquette

www.linkedin.com/advice/1/what-most-important-networking-etiquette-peonf

www.linkedin.com/pulse/how-improve-your-relationship-through-learning-growth-anthony-butcher

www.linkedin.com/pulse/journey-through-time-evolution-communications-tracy-o-clair

www.linkedin.com/pulse/overcome-personal-barriers-during-change-work-how-adkar-wong

www.linkedin.com/pulse/power-authenticity-social-media-more-than-just-jennifer-mcdougall

www.linkedin.com/pulse/power-effective-communication-digital-age-shaik-saleem

www.linkedin.com/pulse/role-mentorship-professional-development-ana-poueriet

www.luther.edu/inside-college-admissions-blog/how-to-embrace-diversity-in-various-forms.

www.marriage.com/advice/relationship/social-media-impact-relationships/

www.masterclass.com/articles/adapting-to-change

www.mayoclinic.org/healthy-lifestyle/adult-health/in-depth/forgiveness/art-20047692

www.medium.com/@bakareayanfe8/invest-time-and-effort-into-your-relationship-f79ce49f130b

www.medium.com/@HaySunny/how-to-set-boundaries-9da630627f27

www.mindbodygreen.com/articles/characteristics-of-healthy-relationships

www.momjunction.com/articles/family-relationship_00460134/

www.ncbi.nlm.nih.gov/pmc/articles/PMC3150158/, https://doi.org/10.1177/0022146510383501

www.npr.org/2022/03/14/1086433752/stay-connected-long-distance-friends

www.ny.gov/teen-dating-violence-awareness-and-prevention/what-does-healthy-relationship-look

www.online.utpb.edu/about-us/articles/communication/how-much-of-communication-is-nonverbal/

www.optimistperformance.com/captains-blog/news/the-power-of-shared-experiences-by-optimist-performance/

www.paigebond.com/blog/self-discovery-strengthening-relationships

www.psychcentral.com/blog/whats-a-toxic-person-how-do-you-deal-with-one#next-steps

www.psychcentral.com/lib/self-esteem-makes-successful-relationships

www.pushfar.com/article/the-roles-and-responsibilities-of-a-mentor/

www.serenitylake.me/how-to-handle-the-challenges-of-long-term-relationships-ccc3ab540de

www.studysmarter.co.uk/explanations/social-studies/social-relationships/#:~:text=Social%20Relationships-

www.thecut.com/article/a-psychologist-explains-how-to-revive-a-dead-friendship.html

www.thedecisionlab.com/biases/halo-effect

www.theparticipationcompany.com/2016/06/5-conflict-resolution-strategies/

www.veretis.com.au/learning-from-different-perspectives/

www.verywellmind.com/6-types-of-relationships-and-their-effect-on-your-life-5209431

www.verywellmind.com/how-to-leave-a-toxic-marriage-4091900

www.verywellmind.com/what-is-self-worth-6543764#:~:text=It

www.vilendrerlaw.com/five-main-causes-conflict-mediation-can-resolve/

www.wellbeingpeople.com/family-wellbeing/what-is-empathy-and-why-is-it-good-for-us/2023/

www.wellnesstogether.ca/en-ca/resource/adapting-to-changing-family-dynamics

www.wikipedia.org/wiki/Shopping_addiction

www.ingramcontent.com/pod-product-compliance
Lightning Source LLC
Chambersburg PA
CBHW060046230426
43661CB00004B/677